and

THE IQ MYTH

M J Bromley

www.booksforschool.eu

AUTUS BOOKS
England, UK
www.booksforschool.eu
Twitter: @AutusBooks

Making KS3 Count First Published in 2016
The IQ Myth First Published in 2012

This Edition First Published in 2016
This Edition © Bromley Education 2016

ISBN-13: **978-1535506564**
ISBN-10: **1535506563**

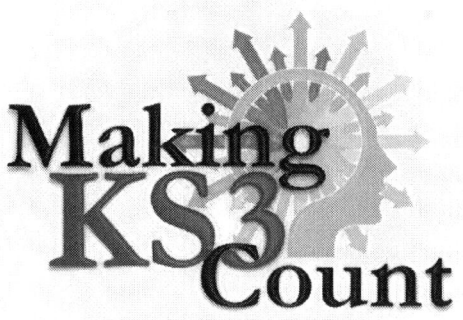

M J Bromley

www.booksforschool.eu

AUTUS BOOKS
England, UK
www.booksforschool.eu
Twitter: @AutusBooks

First Published in 2016

ISBN-13: **978-1535506564**
ISBN-10: **1535506563**

For Henry, Maggie and Meg

Contents

Part One

Introduction

CHAPTER ONE

The Wasted Years?

In the autumn of 2015 Ofsted produced a report entitled Key Stage 3: The Wasted Years? in which it summarised the findings of approximately 1,600 section 5 inspections carried out between September 2013 and March 2015, 318 monitoring inspections carried out between September 2014 and March 2015, 55 section 5 inspections from June and July 2015, 100 interviews with senior leaders, 10,942 questionnaire responses from pupils in Years 7 to 9, and 14 good practice visits.

Rather depressingly, the report found that, while pupils generally had the opportunity to study a broad range of subjects throughout Key Stage 3, in too many schools the quality of teaching and the rate of pupils' progress and achievement were not good enough.

In fact, inspectors reported concerns about the effectiveness of Key Stage 3 in one in five of the routine inspections, particularly in relation to the slow progress made in English and maths and the lack of challenge for the most able pupils. Inspectors also reported significant weaknesses in modern foreign languages

(MFL), history and geography at Key Stage 3. Too often, inspectors found teaching that failed to challenge and engage pupils. Additionally, low-level disruption in some of these lessons, particularly in MFL, had a detrimental impact on pupils' learning. Achievement was not good enough in just under half of the MFL classes observed, two-fifths of the history classes and one third of the geography classes.

The report claimed that the weaknesses inspectors identified in teaching and pupil progress reflect a general lack of priority given to Key Stage 3 by many secondary school leaders. The majority of leaders spoken to as part of the survey, the report said, admitted they staffed Key Stages 4 and 5 before Key Stage 3. As a result, some Key Stage 3 classes were split between more than one teacher or were taught by non-specialists. In this sense - and in the way schools monitor and assess pupils' progress - Key Stage 3 is regarded as a poor relation to the other key stages.

The report also asserted that too many secondary schools did not work effectively with partner primary schools to understand pupils' prior learning and ensure that they built on this during Key Stage 3. Some secondary leaders simply accepted that pupils would repeat what they had already done in primary school during the early part of Key Stage 3, particularly in Year 7. In addition, half of the pupils surveyed said that their homework never, or only some of the time, helped them to make progress. And inspectors found that, too often, homework did not consolidate or extend pupils' learning.

The report claimed that some school leaders did not use the Pupil Premium effectively in Key Stage 3 to ensure that gaps between disadvantaged pupils and their peers continued to close following transition to secondary school. Instead, additional support tended to be focused on intervention activities at Key Stage 4, which by then would have to compensate for ineffective practice in the earlier years of secondary education.

Some of the report's key findings are as follows:

- Key Stage 3 is not a high priority for many secondary school leaders in timetabling, assessment and monitoring of pupils' progress. Eighty five per cent of senior leaders interviewed said that they staff Key Stages 4 and 5 before Key Stage 3. Key Stage 3 is given a lower priority. Classes are often split between more than one teacher and pupils are often taught by non-specialists.
- Leaders prioritise the pastoral over the academic needs of pupils during transition from primary school. While this affects all pupils, it can have a particularly detrimental effect on the progress and engagement of the most able.
- Many secondary schools do not build sufficiently on pupils' prior learning. Many of the senior leaders interviewed said that they do not do this well enough and accepted that some pupils would repeat some of what they had done in Key Stage 2.
- Some school leaders are not using the Pupil Premium funding effectively to close gaps quickly in Key Stage 3. Inspection evidence and senior leaders' comments indicate that this is another area where Key Stage 4 often takes priority.
- Developing pupils' literacy skills in Key Stage 3 is a high priority in many schools but the same level of priority is not given to numeracy. A majority of the headteachers Ofsted spoke to were able to explain how they were improving literacy at Key Stage 3 but only a quarter could do the same for numeracy. This is reflected in inspection evidence, for example from monitoring inspections, where inspectors reported improvements in literacy nearly three times more than they did in numeracy.
- Homework is not consistently providing the opportunities for pupils to consolidate or extend

their learning in Key Stage 3. Approximately half of the pupils who responded to Ofsted's online questionnaire said that their homework never, or only some of the time, helps them to make progress.

In concluding their report, Ofsted recommended senior leaders should make Key Stage 3 a higher priority in all aspects of school planning, monitoring and evaluation, and ensure that not only is the curriculum offer at Key Stage 3 broad and balanced, but that teaching is of a high quality and prepares pupils for more challenging subsequent study at Key Stages 4 and 5.

Ofsted also recommended that senior leaders ensure that transition from Key Stage 2 to 3 focuses as much on pupils' academic needs as it does on their pastoral needs, and that senior leaders foster better cross-phase partnerships with primary schools in order to ensure that Key Stage 3 teachers build on pupils' prior knowledge, understanding and skills.

Ofsted said middle and senior leaders should make sure that systems and procedures for assessing and monitoring pupils' progress in Key Stage 3 are more robust and that leaders should focus on the needs of disadvantaged pupils in Key Stage 3, including the most able, in order to close the achievement gap as quickly as possible. Leaders should also evaluate the quality and effectiveness of homework in Key Stage 3 in order to ensure that it helps pupils to make good progress. And, finally, school leaders should put in place literacy and numeracy strategies that ensure pupils build on their prior attainment in Key Stage 2 in these crucial areas.

All of Ofsted's recommendations are sensible and worthwhile but they are also - perhaps understandably for a high level report - vague and intangible. For example, what does it mean, in reality, to give Key Stage 3 a high priority? What, in practice, do cross-phase partnerships look like? What is robust assessment and monitoring, exactly? And what, precisely, constitutes quality and effective homework?

Over the course of twelve chapters (and two bonus chapters), I will explore these recommendations in greater depth and detail as I seek to offer my own advice on how to lead an effective Key Stage 3 in order to ensure that the three-years of a child's education that constitute Key Stage 3 do not prove to be time wasted but are instead fruitful, enjoyable and rewarding. By the end of this book, I want us to be able to confidently and robustly answer the question that forms the title of Ofsted's report - 'KS3: The Wasted Years?' - with a firm and frank 'no'.

*

The secret to an effective Key Stage 3, I believe, is a better transition process (by which I mean a more effective transition between Key Stages 2 and 3 but also within Key Stage 3 itself as pupils transfer between Years 7, 8 and 9), a better curriculum (by which I mean greater curriculum continuity between the key stages, a curriculum that is challenging, engaging and different to that which precedes and succeeds it, and a curriculum that provides for the effective development of literacy and numeracy skills), better homework (by which I mean homework that enables pupils to practice their learning and provides a real audience, purpose and context), and better assessment (by which I mean the regular monitoring of progress, quality formative feedback, and timely interventions which seek to close the gaps in the performance of different groups of pupils).

As such, my book will be in four distinct parts focusing on:

1. Transition
2. Curriculum
3. Homework
4. Assessment

Part Two

Transition

CHAPTER TWO

Year 6 to 7 transition

Why do we need to improve Year 6 to 7 transition?

According to Galton (1999), almost forty per cent of children fail to make expected progress during the year immediately following a change of schools and DfE data from 2011 shows that average progress drops between Key Stage 2 and Key Stage 3 for reading, writing and maths. Moreover, the effects of transition are amplified by risk factors such as poverty and ethnicity.

Why should this be? Primarily, it's because there is insufficient or ineffective communication between primary and secondary schools. This has a number of harmful consequences.

Firstly, secondary school teachers have a weak understanding of the curriculum content that precedes that which they personally teach whilst primary school teachers have a weak understanding of the curriculum that succeeds their own. In practice, this means that the curriculum is not joined up and that pupils are taught content and skills more than once or are taught the same concepts in contradictory ways.

Secondly, assessment practices in the two phases are inconsistent and therefore there is little correlation between Year 6 and 7 data. This leads to a lack of trust on both sides of the 'divide' in terms of the validity of assessment data and to pupils being re-tested at the start of Year 7 just weeks after sitting stressful, high stakes Key Stage 2 SATs. It also generates confusion and even animosity amongst parents who perceive that their sons and daughters are regressing when in fact the data may mask their progress or, at any rate, exaggerate the decline.

Thirdly, and in part a further consequence of the first two points above but also the result of pedagogical differences between the two phases, there is often a weak understanding in Year 7 of what pupils can achieve and therefore insufficient challenge in the curriculum.

How can we improve transition?

There are five key realms of school life - sometimes referred to as transition 'bridges' - in which the transition process can be improved:

1. Administrative
2. Social and personal
3. Curricular
4. Pedagogic
5. Managing learning

The *administrative* 'bridge' is concerned with the general management of the transition process such as the formal liaison between a secondary school and its feeder primaries, usually at a senior leadership level. In practice, this might take the form of the transfer of pupil records and achievement data, meetings with pupils and parents, and visits from headteachers, senior leaders and teachers.

The **social and personal** 'bridge' is concerned with forging links between pupils/parents and their new school prior to and immediately after transfer. It is also concerned with the pupil induction process into their new school and might take the form of induction days, open evenings, school orientation activities, team-building days, taster classes, the production and issuing of prospectuses and booklets, and so on.

The **curricular** 'bridge' is concerned with improving curriculum continuity between the primary and secondary phases of education by sharing plans that show what content is taught on either side of the transition. This involves teachers rather than senior leaders and might take the form of cross-phase teaching, the teaching of bridging units at the end of Year 6 and start of Year 7, summer schools, joint CPD networks and INSET days, the sharing of good practice and shared planning, and teacher exchanges.

Whereas the curricular bridge is concerned with what pupils are taught, the **pedagogic** 'bridge' is concerned with establishing a shared understanding of how pupils are taught - as well as how they learn - in order to achieve a greater continuity in classroom practice and teaching. This is achieved by understanding differing teaching styles and skills, by engaging in shared CPD and teacher exchanges, and by primary and secondary teachers observing each other in practice.

The **managing learning** 'bridge' is about ensuring that pupils are active participants, rather than passive observers, in the transition process. This is achieved by empowering pupils and their parents with information about achievement and empowering them with the confidence to articulate their learning needs in a new environment. This might take the form of giving information to parents/pupils, providing pupils with learning portfolios and samples of achievements, and raising pupils' awareness of their needs and talents by sharing and explaining data.

What is the success criteria?

There are three measures of an effective transition process:

1. Social adjustment
2. Institutional adjustment
3. Curriculum interest and continuity

Social adjustment is about pupils successfully making new friends and reporting higher self-esteem.

Institutional adjustment is about pupils settling in well at their new school and getting used to their new school's routines, systems and structures.

Curriculum interest and continuity is about pupils being prepared for the level and style of work they encounter at secondary school, as well as being appropriately challenged and engaged, and building on the progress they made at primary school.

How can we achieve it?

In practice, we can improve the transition process and achieve social adjustment, institutional adjustment and curriculum interest and continuity by employing some or all of the following strategies:

Firstly, we can actively engage Year 7 pupils in group and pair work and use seating plans to help them make friends.

Secondly, we can take Year 7 pupils out of school either during the summer or at the start of the autumn term for team-building activities and residential trips.

Thirdly, we can have a staggered start to the year so that Year 7 are alone in the school building for a day or so and can familiarise themselves with the geography and routines without being overwhelmed or frightened by the busyness of the corridors. We can also have staggered breaks and lunches for a week or so to enable pupils to have quiet 'play' with friends and to have a more leisurely lunch in a safe environment and without extensive queuing.

Fourthly, we can arrange regular visits from secondary school teachers to Year 6 to talk about life in 'big school' and, perhaps an even more impactful strategy, we can arrange for regular visits from Year 7 pupils to talk to Year 6 and share their experiences of the transition process and of life after transition. Pupils are more likely to listen to their peers than they are to their teachers and will be relieved to hear from pupils in the year above them that life in 'big school' isn't quite as daunting as they think.

Finally, feeder primary schools can operate an open door policy for parents to air any concerns and questions. Secondary schools, meanwhile, can hold a parents' evening in the summer term to welcome new parents and answer questions about the transition and induction process, and a further parents' evening in the autumn term for 'settling in' discussions and to talk to their child's form tutor.

What might this look like in practice?

Let's take a look at an imaginary transition process starting in Year 5, working through to Year 7...

Year 5

Transition should not begin in the summer term of Year 6. It needs to begin much earlier in order to effective. In Year 5, for example, there might be specialist visits and workshops led by secondary teachers from various curriculum areas. These not only provide pupils with a flavour of the subject specialisms and teacher expertise they would otherwise be denied but also enable pupils to familiarise themselves with their future teachers and their teaching styles.

Also in Year 5, the headteacher of the secondary school might provide a tour of their school during the day in order to provide pupils with the experience of 'big school' and allay some of the fears that inevitably fester as the rumour mill begins to grind. Other senior leaders, particularly the leader responsible for transition and the SENCO, might pay regular visits to primary schools to talk to pupils and meet with parents. And there might be ongoing close liaison between Year 5 and Year 6 teachers within the primary school in order to identify children who might potentially experience issues around transition. The school might then identify key opportunities within the Year 6 curriculum to support the development of the requisite skills these vulnerable pupils will need in order to survive and thrive in secondary school.

Year 6

Autumn Term
In the autumn term of Year 6, there might be forums in which the transition programme is shared with pupils and there is an opportunity to answer pupils' questions. This might be followed by open days and information evenings at secondary school for prospective pupils and their parents. Parents may also request additional meetings with leaders and teachers from the secondary school such as the SENCO. Also in the autumn term, parents will complete an on-line application form for the secondary schools of their choice so primary schools might need to provide support during this process.

Spring Term
In the spring term of Year 6, secondary schools will receive a list of admissions and parents will receive

confirmation of their child's place. Transfer forms will be sent to feeder primary schools to gather information on all pupils. Primary schools will need to gather permission from their Year 6 pupils in order to attach one-page profiles to their transfer forms. Primary and secondary staff might then liaise in order to discuss pupils' strengths, interests and possible support needs.

Secondary staff might also visit their primary feeder schools in order to talk with Year 6 pupils about their proposed transition programme and to receive information from pupils, parents and staff, as well as offer opportunities for discussion. Year 7 pupils might visit primary schools to speak to Year 6 about their recent experience of transition and answer questions in order to allay any fears. At this stage, staff might identify vulnerable pupils and put in place a raft of additional support with the transition process, including, perhaps, a dedicated teaching assistant for transition.

A letter might be sent to parents/carers to inform them of their child's inclusion in specialist transition work. Small groups of vulnerable pupils might begin meeting their transition worker on a regular basis.

Summer Term
In the summer term of Year 6, there might be a pupil and parent/carer consultation on transition procedures and a further open evening to provide parents with an opportunity to meet key staff such as their child's head of year, form tutor, SENCO, the school nurse, the school's caterers, the head boy and head girl, and so on. Parents might also be invited to make fifteen minute appointments with their child's form tutor for June/July and use the opportunity to visit their child's new classroom. The summer term might also provide opportunities for parents to purchase new uniform.

Also in the summer term, the secondary school SENCO and possibly an EAL teacher might provide summaries on high needs children in the Year 6 cohort for their secondary colleagues alongside the one-page profiles which include information on 'how best to support me' written by the child. The one-page profiles might then be reviewed and updated by pupils and their teachers.

There might also be Year 6 pupil transfer days in which pupils visit their secondary schools and take part in sample lessons, experience the lunchtime routine and take part in an orientation activity to get to know their way around the school building and grounds.

Curriculum areas might begin planning transition projects to be taught in the autumn term. A letter of introduction might be written by the headteacher or senior leader responsible for transition and sent to all Year 6 pupils. A tutor meeting with parents and pupils might take place in which the home-school agreement is discussed and signed. And a prospectus and transition booklet might be given to the pupils.

Year 7
In the autumn term of Year 7, the secondary school will welcome new pupils and this might involve a staggered start to the year in which only Year 7 are present on the first day and in which breaks and lunches are staggered for the first week to allow new pupils some space and freedom to become familiar and comfortable with the buildings and routines. There might also be an alternative timetable for the first week and a series of transition activities such as team-building events or cross-curricular projects to develop key skills. There might also be a parents' evening in order to outline the transition arrangements and afford parents the opportunity to meet their chid's form tutor and head of year, as well as to familiarise themselves with the new school.

Additional support for vulnerable children

In addition to the transition process outlined above, a school might decide to appoint a Teaching Assistant dedicated to transition in order to support vulnerable pupils. Below I outline what they might do.

Spring Term
The Teaching Assistant (TA) for Transition might visit their feeder primary schools with a member of the Senior Leadership Team to meet staff, pupils and parents and outline their role and responsibilities, how the vulnerable pupils have been identified, what support will be offered and why. They might also meet Year 6 teachers to take suggestions for further referrals. They might then establish their groups and book dates for the summer term.

Summer Term
The TA might meet individual pupils in their primary school setting and take groups of pupils (say 6-8) on visits to their secondary school on a number of occasions over the course of the summer term. These groups and visits may be mixed with pupils from other primary schools in order to help pupils make new friends. The programme might be based around concerns and issues raised by the children and what practical strategies will support them in secondary school and may also include some generic coping strategies and soft skills (see below).

Autumn and Spring Terms
The TA might continue to work with their identified children. If the initial groups were each from single primary schools, the TA might now decide to amalgamate some or all of them. The TA will continue to listen to pupils and be responsive to their concerns.

Some practical skills for survival:
- What is a friend/a real friend/making friends?
- Packing a bag the night before
- Avoiding bullies
- Who might be the most important person?
- What would I do if........? (problem solving)

- What is Homework Club?
- Being a good listener
- Using your leisure time
- How do I make my work more successful?

*

What can we do to improve parents' engagement with the transition process?

To conclude this chapter on the transition between Key Stages 2 and 3, I'd like to explore in greater detail the issue of parental engagement.

Above, I said that the social and personal 'bridge' is concerned with forging links between a school and its pupils and their parents prior to and immediately after transfer. I went on to say that, in order to make a success of transition, feeder primary schools should operate an open door policy for parents to air any concerns and questions whilst secondary schools should hold parents' evenings in the summer and autumn terms. But what more can be done to ensure that the communication between schools and parents is effective and why does this matter..?

A MetLife survey in 2005 said that the biggest challenge faced by new teachers was engaging with and involving parents. MetLife research from 2012 suggests that, although home-school communications have improved over the last twenty-five years or so, parental engagement continues to be an area of improvement for most schools.

And yet parental engagement is of great import in all sorts of ways. For example, according to Butler et el (2008), Haynes et al (1989), and Henderson (1987), it is associated with higher academic achievement. Butler et el (2008) and Haynes et al (1989) also claim that effective parental engagement leads to increased rates of pupil attendance whilst Becher (1984) and Henderson et al (1986) say it can have a positive effect on students' attitudes to learning as well as on their behaviour. Research has also shown that getting communication with parents right can lead to an increased level of interest in pupils' work (see, for example, Rich [1988] and Tobolka [2006]), increased parent satisfaction with their child's teachers (see Rich [1988]), and higher rates of teacher satisfaction (see MetLife [2012]).

So the big question now is how can we improve parental engagement at Key Stage 3 and, in particular, with regards the transition process?

Firstly, communication needs to start early and continue throughout the transition process. The parents of pupils moving from Year 6 to Year 7 will not want to receive information halfway through the summer holidays at which point it will be deemed too late. Schools need to engage with parents early and clearly set out their expectations and requirements.

Secondly, communication needs to be a two-way process: as well as the school staying in touch with parents, parents also need a means of keeping in contact with the school throughout the transition process. One way to do this is to create an FAQ page, as well as a Q&A facility and a forum on the school's website.

Thirdly, one way to ensure communications are appropriately timed, relevant and useful is to utilise the experience and expertise of current Year 7 pupils and their parents. For example, the parents of current Year 7 pupils will be able to share their thoughts on *what* information they needed when they went through the transition process with their child not so long ago, as well as *when* they needed it most, whilst current Year 7 pupils will be able to offer their advice about how to prepare for secondary school by, to give but two examples, providing a reading list for the summer and sharing their advice about how to get ready for the first day of school.

Fourthly, communication should take myriad forms and should embrace new and emerging technologies.

The use of technologies such as email, texting, websites, electronic portfolios and online assessment and reporting tools have - accordingly to Merkley, Schmidt, Dirksen and Fuhler (2006) - made communication between parents and teachers more timely, efficient, productive and satisfying.

So what might the use of technology to communicate with parents look like in practice? Here are a few suggestions for how technology could be used to help you communicate with parents and, indeed, vice versa:

- Parents could send teachers an email to let them know when the home learning environment may be (temporarily or otherwise) holding a pupil back.
- Likewise, teachers could send parents an email to let them know when issues arise at school which may have a detrimental effect on the pupil, such as noticeable changes in behaviour or deficits in academic performance.
- Teachers could text parents at the end of the day on which a student has done something particularly well or shown real progress or promise. Instant and personal feedback like this is really valuable and helps make a connection between the teacher and a child's parents.
- Teachers could send half-termly or monthly newsletters via email to parents to inform them about which topics they are covering in class in the coming weeks, what homework will be set and when, and how parents can help.
- The school could use text, email and the school website to keep parents updated on forthcoming field trips, parent association meetings and other school activities.

- Teachers could use email to send out regular tips to parents on how they might be able to support their child's learning that week/month. For example, they could send a list of questions to ask their child about what students have been learning in class. They could also send hyperlinks to interactive quizzes or games.
- The school could use the school website to gather more frequent and informal parent voice feedback about specific topics. For example, they might post a short survey after each open evening and parents' evening.
- The school could provide an online calendar via its website to allow parents to volunteer to help in class, say as reading mentors or helpers at special events.
- An online calendar could also be used as a booking facility to enable parents to make their own meetings with school staff rather than having to phone the school, which many people find daunting.
- The online calendar could prove useful for booking slots at parents' evenings and other open evenings and events, enabling parents to be in control of the times at which they attend school rather than relying on a child and their teachers to agree suitable slots.

Improving parental engagement is not without its challenges, of course. Here are a few barriers you will need to consider and overcome if you are to increase the effectiveness of your communications with parents and, as a consequence, improve the transition process for pupils entering Key Stage 3:

1. Parents might perceive the school as presenting obstacles in the form of a lack of encouragement, not informing parents of what they can do, and having too little scope for fitting around busy working and family lives.

2. Parents might face numerous barriers to engagement, including costs, time and transportation, language (for

some parents for whom English is not a first language), low levels of literacy and numeracy, and a lack of confidence in supporting children's learning or engaging with a school.

3. Sustainability might be an issue, in particular retaining committed and inspiring senior leaders, high levels of commitment across staff teams, and access to the funding streams and resources that successful programmes require.

4. Reaching and involving parents who have chosen not to engage either with their children's school or with their children's learning might be a challenge.

5. Lack of staff experience and knowledge of working to support parents in engaging with their children's learning might be a barrier.

To conclude this chapter, I'll share the recommendations of a 2010 Department for Education review of best practice in parental engagement. The report recommended that schools develop a parental engagement strategy which contains the following key features:

1. *Planning* - parental engagement must be planned for and embedded in the whole school strategy. The planning cycle should include a comprehensive needs analysis; the establishment of mutual priorities; ongoing monitoring and evaluation of interventions; and a public awareness process to help parents and teachers understand and commit to a strategic plan.

2. *Leadership* - effective leadership of parental engagement is essential to the success of programmes and strategies. A parental engagement programme is often led by a senior leader, although leadership may also be distributed in the context of a programme or cluster of schools and services working to a clear strategic direction.

3. *Collaboration and engagement* - parental engagement requires active collaboration with parents and should be proactive rather than reactive. It should be sensitive to the circumstances of all families, recognise the contributions parents can make, and aim to empower parents.

4. *Sustained improvement* - a parental engagement strategy should be the subject of ongoing support, monitoring and development. This will include strategic planning which embeds parental engagement in whole-school development plans, sustained support, resourcing and training, community involvement at all levels of management, and a continuous system of evidence based development and review.

*

In Chapter Three I will examine the transition between the three years within Key Stage 3, in particular the transition into Year 8 where pupils experience a dip in motivation and progress.

CHAPTER THREE

Avoiding the Year 8 'dip'

In Chapter One I summarised Ofsted's 2015 report KS3: The Wasted Years? which claims that Key Stage 3 is not a high priority for many secondary school leaders in timetabling, assessment and the monitoring of pupils' progress and that school leaders prioritise the pastoral over the academic needs of pupils during transition from primary school. The report also says that many secondary schools do not build sufficiently on pupils' prior learning. Some school leaders, Ofsted state, are not using the Pupil Premium funding effectively to close gaps quickly in Key Stage 3 and, although developing pupils' literacy skills in Key Stage 3 is a high priority in many schools, the same level of priority is not given to numeracy. Finally, the report claims that homework in Key Stage 3 is not consistently providing pupils with the opportunities to consolidate or extend their learning.

Ofsted made a series of recommendations which, whilst sensible and worthwhile, are also vague and intangible. These chapters, therefore, are my attempt to offer advice on how to lead an effective Key Stage 3 and ensure that those three-years of a child's education do not prove to be time wasted but are instead fruitful, enjoyable and rewarding. By the end of this book, I want us to confidently and robustly answer the question that forms the title of Ofsted's report - KS3: The Wasted Years? - with a firm and frank 'no'.

The secret to an effective Key Stage 3, I believe, is a better transition process, a better curriculum, better homework, and better assessment. In the first chapter of this book I examined why improving the transition between primary and secondary schools was so important.

In Chapter Two, I explained how to improve the transition process and what an effective transition might look like in practice. In this chapter I will turn my attention to transition in its wider sense because transition is not just about the move from Year 6 into Year 7, from one Key Stage to another. Indeed, it is about the various movements within a Key Stage, too; particularly from Year 7 into Year 8 which is often regarded as a stop-gap year. And it is also about establishing longer term, more sustainable cross-phase partnerships between primary and secondary schools in order to make transition feel seamless, smooth and natural.

Let's now explore the transition of pupils from Year 7 into Year 8...

Transition within a key stage

Year 7 is new and exciting, if not a little daunting; Year 9 assumes a higher status because its curriculum often includes elective subjects, it comes at the end of a key stage and carries with it national tests (albeit now optional) and GCSE options or, in some schools, signals the start of a three-year Key Stage 4. Year 8, however, which is awkwardly sandwiched between them, is often seen as a stop-gap, wandering alone and confused in the wilderness.

In Year 8 there are no tests of any great import, no big decisions to make, and nothing is particularly new or exciting anymore. New school is now old hat. What's more, it's often the year in which pupils' hormones begin to rage. As a result, towards the end of Year 7 and during Year 8, pupils begin to get demotivated and their progress slows or stalls.

If you Google 'Year 8 dip' you'll find plenty of frustrated patter in parents' forums as mums and dads ask if it's normal for their son or daughter to be so demotivated at school and to be stalling in their studies. The responses they garner are invariably reassuring: yes, it's perfectly normal and a perennial problem in schools. But aside from the chatroom chatter, there is precious little research or advice on how to tackle this phenomenon. So how can we avoid this 'dip'?

Well, as is often the case, I find the solution lies in the problem. If the problem is that Year 8 isn't regarded as new or exciting, then we need to make it feel new and exciting. If the problem is that Year 8 is the year in which pupils usually start puberty and their hormones kick in with a vengeance as they begin the journey towards maturity, then we need to recognise this increasing maturity. If the problem is that Year 8, without tests and options, is regarded as meaningless, as a stop-gap, then we need to make it feel meaningful and use assessment and feedback to motivate pupils to make better progress.

So here are my top tips for avoiding the Year 8 'dip' and ensuring that the transition from Year 7 into Year 8 is just as smooth and effective as we hope the transition from primary to secondary proved to be...

Make each year special and have a curriculum that ensures progression and continuity. We need to ensure that Year 8 is different to Year 7 and Year 9, that it offers something unique, challenging and engaging. This might be in the form of cross-curricular project-based learning but whatever approach to the curriculum we take we must make sure that Year 8 represents a significant step-change in terms of difficulty and complexity.

Notwithstanding the importance of spaced practice (of repeating learning several times and leaving increasingly long gaps before returning to re-test), what Year 8 must not do is unnecessarily repeat curriculum content from primary school and Year 7. In order to ensure Year 8 offers something new, Year 7 and Year 8 teachers, if they are different, must closely liaise on their curriculum planning to achieve continuity.

Another way to make Year 8 feel special is to take advantage of the freedom afforded by its lack of formal testing and qualifications and pack it full of extra-curricular opportunities such as educational visits, residential trips, and so on. Serve a rich diet of culture - in or out of school - with theatre productions and museum visits, healthy eating expos and sporting events, science fairs and art and design competitions and exhibitions. Really bring learning to life.

Of course, money is always a consideration but we must take Ofsted's advice and make better use of the Pupil Premium funding in Key Stage 3 rather than stockpile it for Key Stage 4 interventions. If we use more of it in Year 8 (and therefore less at GCSE) - in conjunction with other funding streams - in order to ensure that all pupils get fair access to enrichment opportunities, then they will be motivated and make better progress, hence they will commence their GCSEs from a more advantageous starting point and far fewer remedial interventions will be needed in Years 10 and 11.

Recognise the increasing maturity of pupils. We need to ensure that pupils - who are starting to experience puberty and grow into young adults - feel that their increasing maturity is being recognised and appreciated.

To do this, we need to make Year 8 pupils feel set apart from Year 7 but only in the best sense. Rather than setting Year 8 in opposition to Year 7 we should utilise their maturity and experience to support, advise and mentor the new cohort of pupils. Year 8 pupils could be trained as reading mentors, for example, or as break and lunchtime 'buddies' and guides. They could play a big role during the Year 7 induction.

We tend to favour much older pupils in these roles - and not without good reason as sixth form students are mature, more accomplished readers, and in need of supporting evidence for their UCAS applications - but older students are also busy with important exams whereas Year 8 have the time to spare and need to feel valued. They are also more able to empathise with their Year 7 peers, being closer in age and having more recently experienced transition and induction.

We could also recognise the increasing maturity of Year 8 pupils by tweaking our rewards and sanctions policy, ensuring that rewards remain age-appropriate and motivational, and that sanctions continue to be suitably punitive but not demeaning. Ideally, we should involve Year 8 pupils in this process by consulting them on what the rewards and sanctions should be - the very process of consultation, whatever the outcome, will make them feel valued and mature.

Have systems that recognise and correct disaffection early, and provide opportunities for a fresh start. As well as ensuring our rewards and sanctions policy remains relevant as pupils grow in maturity, we need to make sure that low-level disruption and general disaffection - which are prevalent in Year 8 - are spotted early and tackled effectively. Those systems need to be positive and motivating, giving pupils a reason to reassert themselves and work hard. The key, again, is in an effective rewards policy but also in the use of intrinsic rewards, the reward of learning itself not extrinsic rewards such as prizes.

In order for pupils to feel rewarded by learning and achieving, we need them to believe that their work has a genuine audience and purpose. Pupils also need to feel that they have some ownership of the work - both in terms of the content and format, and in terms of how it will be assessed.

Perhaps most importantly, any system that seeks to recognise and correct disaffection and low level disruption must make clear that there is a way back. Pupils need to be afforded a fresh start. This applies to pupils who may have misbehaved or underachieved in Year 7 who now need to know - explicitly and implicitly - that Year 8 represents a new start for them and an opportunity to make amends, and to pupils who let themselves down during Year 8 but need a way back before they start Year 9.

Have pastoral systems that support pupils in their learning as well as their behaviour. We need to make sure that our pastoral systems do not focus solely on pupils' behaviour and wellbeing - as is often the case in the early years of Key Stage 3. We must not neglect pupils' academic needs. In practice, this means providing support for pupils whose behaviour is good but who need support either over the long-term or at key waypoints on their learning journey. This might be in the form of in-class support or extra sessions, or it might be in the form of differentiated learning such as differentiated questioning, a choice of outcomes or the application of mastery learning approaches.

Regularly evaluate progress and have effective intervention plans. We need to ensure that Year 8 isn't a wasted year filled with 'fluff' assignments and meaningless assessments. We need to set meaningful work that will stretch and challenge pupils and then assess their progress regularly and accurately so that they can be given detailed formative feedback on which they can act and improve. In short, we should ensure that we put in place the same robust assessment, monitoring and tracking systems in Year 8 that we use for our GCSE and A Level students.

In practice, this means that pupil progress is regularly observed and analysed and that the data is shared with all interested parties - parents, staff and governors. This means that the data is used in a number of ways including to identify underperforming groups, to direct the appropriate deployment of staff and resources, to inform target-setting, to monitor the impact of strategies and interventions, and to challenge the aspirations and assumptions of pupils, parents and staff. This also means having in place a well-developed pupil tracking system to capture a wider range of data in addition to attainment levels, and using external data and self-evaluation in order to focus on gaps and progress, not just average attainment. And it means that attainment data, as well as informing staff on pupil progress, is used to provide pupils with regular feedback on their progress.

In Chapter Four we will examine the importance of establishing longer-term cross-phase partnerships between early years, primary and secondary schools.

CHAPTER FOUR

Cross-phase partnerships

So far in this book I've summarised Ofsted's report KS3: The Wasted Years? which claims that Key Stage 3 is not a high priority for many secondary school leaders in timetabling, assessment and the monitoring of pupils' progress and that school leaders prioritise the pastoral over the academic needs of pupils during transition from primary school. The report also says that many secondary schools do not build sufficiently on pupils' prior learning, that some school leaders are not using the Pupil Premium funding effectively to close gaps quickly in Key Stage 3 and that homework does not consistently provide opportunities for pupils to consolidate or extend their learning.

In the first chapter in this book I examined why improving the transition between primary and secondary schools was so important. In the second chapter I explained what an effective transition looked like in practice and how we can achieve it. In the third chapter I turned my attention to the transition pupils experience when they move from year to year within a key stage, most notably from Year 7 into Year 8 which is known for a dip in pupil motivation and progress.

In this chapter I will explore how to develop more lasting and sustainable cross-phase partnerships between primary and secondary schools.

*

Making a pupil's transition from Key Stage 2 to Key Stage 3 smooth and effective takes more than just a little team-work at the end of Year 6 and the beginning of Year 7. Indeed, even starting the process in Year 5 as I suggested in an earlier chapter is not really sufficient. Rather, what is needed is long-term, genuine and sustainable collaboration between schools. We need early years, primary and secondary schools to work in close partnership on all aspects of a child's education, sharing information and resources, in order to ensure that each child is well-protected and experiences a continuity of service and support.

Why do we need better collaboration? Because projects that link up pupils, teachers and schools across early years, primary and secondary phases can have a positive impact on pupils and teachers by supporting pupils to experience a smoother transition and make continuous progress both academically and in terms of their soft skills, and by enabling teachers and schools to learn from best practice across different stages of the system.

So what might this collaboration look like in practice? It might involve all phases of compulsory education establishing family links, sharing services such as family liaison officers, education welfare officers, SENCOs, EAL teachers and other specialists. It might involve all phases jointly planning and running projects and events such as summer schools or careers fairs. It might take the form of joint curriculum planning. It might take the form of joint CPD networks and INSET days, and teacher visits and exchanges. It might also involve cross-phase mentoring and tutoring.

Whatever form it takes in practice - and I will explore more examples in a moment - it is important, as much as is possible, to see the two phases as one, particularly to see Years 5 through to 8 as a single phase when it comes to planning the curriculum because this will help to bridge the primary/secondary divide. Planning a unique 'middle years' curriculum will also help to combat the problem of Key Stage 3 - particularly Year 8 - being seen as 'wasted years' and a poor relation to GCSE. Indeed, it will give it identify and purpose.

Whilst we're on this topic, what will also help to bridge the divide - and one of the desired outcomes of an effective cross-phase partnership - is encouraging pupils to bring in their best work from each subject in primary school when they start secondary. This work can then be affixed to the front of pupils' exercise books in Year 7 to remind them and their teachers what they're capable of producing. Such a tactic will help combat the common complaint that secondary teachers underestimate pupils' abilities and that pupils' standards slide following transition.

Another desired outcome of an effective cross-phase partnership is to ensure that all Year 6 and 7 teachers work together to familiarise each other with the National Curriculum of the phase they teach as well as the secondary school's own curriculum and the school curriculum for the main feeder primaries.

Cross-phase partnerships can also be fruitfully employed designing 'settling-in' sessions and summer schools for pupils but these should have an academic rather than pastoral flavour. Primary and secondary colleagues could also work together to design formative and summative assessment strategies which make it easier for teachers to track pupils' progress as they move out of one phase and into the next.

Where possible, cross-phase partnerships could enable

teachers to work across the different phases in order to introduce more subject-specialist teaching to the later years of primary school as well as encourage a more holistic approach to pupils' development at the beginning of Key Stage 3.

Primary school leaders play a crucial role in making cross-phase partnerships work. Firstly, they need to set clear expectations for their staff about the importance of sharing and communicating with their secondary colleagues by encouraging teachers to help pupils produce transition 'passports' which showcase both their academic and their broader achievements at primary school. Secondary school leaders play an equally important role. For example, they need to encourage Year 7 teachers who are struggling to understand a particular pupil's needs to consider contacting their old Year 6 teacher for a conversation.

Multi-academy trusts that encompass secondaries and some of their feeder primaries have an advantage when it comes to cross-phase partnerships and many are already ahead of the curve. Their shared HR and payroll structures and systems enable greater and easier collaboration. For example, in cross-phase MATs it is possible to employ teachers who work across the primary and secondary phases. This might mean that Year 6 teachers move up with their classes and teach them in Year 7, thus making the transition much less daunting.

It is also possible to have cross-phase subject leaders so that, for example, a Director of English oversees the MAT's English provision from Reception right through to A Level and perhaps has a Subject Leader for each phase but the phases do not follow the traditional pattern but straddle the key stage divide such as the 'middle years' of Years 5 to 8. The same could be said of pastoral leaders, too, with a Pastoral Leader of Years 5, 6 and 7 rather than the traditional Key Stage 3. And senior leader roles could also be designed to ensure that assessment, for example, as well as, say, the curriculum and pedagogy, are joined up and continuous across all phases.

*

In Wales, an experiment in cross-phase partnerships has led to improvements in pupil outcomes and the raising of standards of educational practice and attainment. NFER researchers analysed twenty schools – four matched pairs of secondary schools and six of primary schools - who were involved in the experiments in 2016 and found that most of the schools believed their partnerships had improved standards of teaching and learning, and had raised pupil performance in maths and numeracy.

The NFER also found evidence that leadership at both senior and middle levels had been enhanced as a result of cross-phase partnerships and that schools' data tracking and assessment systems had been strengthened.

Most of the staff who were interviewed noted the positive impact of the partnerships, and particularly praised the "mutual trust, willingness and respect between the schools which had facilitated effective collaboration". However, they also admitted that there were some factors which might have constrained the relationships, including proximity and differences in pupils, cohorts and characteristics.

One headteacher involved in the project told NFER researchers: "The key for us in the beginning was trust and we are now in the situation where we are very open with each other, friendly ... it was about developing relationships, going slowly, getting to know each other and having the confidence to be open and honest."

Teachers who were involved in the project reported that they had refined approaches to teaching and learning, which had had a big impact on the work done. Teachers felt more confident to try different approaches and to experiment with techniques that they may not have used previously. As a result, lessons become more dynamic and interactive, inviting pupils to become active participants. The quality of feedback improved and teachers changed the way they asked questions, allowing them to elicit answers which delved into how well learners understood concepts and issues.

Some schools had also used the partnerships to look at how they might deliver the curriculum more effectively, including focusing on literacy and numeracy. Teachers told the NFER that being involved in a partnership had made them more reflective of their own practice, and that they had looked at different ways of learning. This included examining how they used data as part of teaching and learning to suit the individual needs of classes of individual pupils.

In secondary schools, most heads and teachers said that participation in the partnership had had a positive effect on teaching, with one senior leader describing it as a "journey of improvement". Teachers said that they had more opportunities to self-evaluate their own classroom practice and were developing an "extended repertoire of teaching, assessment and tracking skills". This was achieved by discussing different methods and approaches, sharing schemes of work and methods of tracking and using data, as well as lesson observations. Teachers also said they had gained the skills to teach smaller classes and of working with individual pupils.

The NFER report said: "Most senior leaders and teachers considered that classroom practice was improving as a result of the increased interaction between staff within and between schools, which had raised staff awareness of alternative approaches when planning, teaching and assessing."

At the whole-school level, one primary or secondary school in the partnership often influenced how things were done in the other. Headteachers became more reflective of their own leadership styles and in some cases, leadership teams were restructured as a result of the partnership. There were also changes among some middle leadership teams, with some middle leaders taking on new responsibilities.

The use of data was also strengthened, with schools changing how they collected data and how they then used this to support teaching and learning, in particular in supporting individual pupils. NFER researchers noted that in some partnerships staff raised their expectations of what learners could achieve. At the same time, pupils were made more aware of their targets and the level at which they should be working. This had the knock-on effect of making them reflect on their own needs, even setting down their own success criteria. Partnership schools used pupils' work from both settings to standardise judgments for assessment and moderation. In some cases, work from one school was adapted for use in the other.

However, what did not work was an approach based on transferring practice directly from one school to another, or where school leaders assumed that what worked in their school would be effective practice elsewhere. As a result of all this, the NFER found that: "Learners' motivation improved and they were more engaged with teachers and the learning process. All of these changes were related to work to strengthen learners' voices, through formal processes for them to make their views known about their own learning and other work to nurture their independence and their enjoyment of their work."

The most lasting changes, researchers found, came about when there was a shift in attitude and culture, and this was needed alongside structural and procedural changes if reforms were to work.

The partnerships appear to have helped schools to make sustained improvements. The study concluded that the partnerships had been effective in supporting and speeding up changes in participating schools. This was achieved partly through matching up schools effectively, the support that was given by the government, and the 'emotional intelligence' shown by senior leaders in getting their staff on board with the project while being mindful of their emotions and sensibilities.

You can read the NFER report in full on their website at www.nfer.ac.uk

In Part Three we will consider ways to improve the Key Stage 3 curriculum so that it is both challenging and engaging.

Part Three

Curriculum

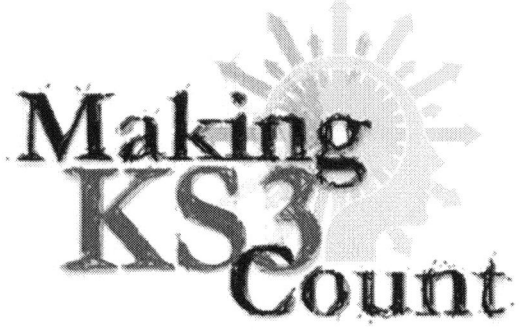

CHAPTER FIVE

Curriculum collaboration

One of the advantages of the kinds of cross-phase partnership I explored in Chapter Four is the opportunity for primary and secondary colleagues to collaborate on curriculum planning in order to ensure a joined up approach so that work is not repeated. Another way of ensuring the curriculum flows between the two phases is for primary and secondary teachers to design a 'bridging' unit that links the end of Year 6 with the beginning of Year 7. This has several advantages. Not only do pupils see the explicit link between the two phases and therefore feel less daunted by the perceived 'divide' between the two, they are also able to start the new year at an advantage, with prior knowledge of a subject and with ready-made work to show their new teacher what they're capable of achieving.

Another advantage of cross-phase partnerships related to the curriculum is the opportunity to share data in order to ensure that pupils' prior attainment is used to set groups and to plan teaching so that lessons provide appropriate challenge. This helps avoid the common criticism that Year 7 often repeats work that pupils did in

Year 6 or is too easy. And it helps Year 7 teachers to differentiate effectively.

But data is more than just a spreadsheet, it is a conversation...

Most secondary teachers will already have access to some information about their new Year 7s including which primary school they came from, the scaled scores they achieved on their Key Stage 2 tests and, if they delve into the question level analysis available, the marks they received for individual questions in those tests. But a pupil's Year 6 teacher will know so much more than these numbers can possibly tell us. They'll know, for example, what the pupil is capable of achieving when they're not under test conditions and what particular topics they've studied and found interesting. They'll know what their attitude to learning is like and what skills they've developed over their first seven years of schooling. They'll know what extra-curricular activities they've taken part in and how well they did, as well as what motivates them to succeed and what demotivates them. They'll know, too, what their home life is like and what obstacles they've had to overcome and might still be facing on a daily basis.

So, yes, data is more than a spreadsheet. And cross-phase partnerships and shared curriculum planning enables data to become a rich and meaningful conversation.

As well as *what* is taught, cross-phase partnerships can ensure that - when it comes to the curriculum - teachers from primary and secondary schools liaise on *how* it is taught. A partnership might, for example, set up a primary/secondary CPD network in order to ensure that approaches to pedagogy are better matched and that teachers from both phases learn from each other about what works in the classroom and about what motivates pupils and how pupils learn. It's important for teachers on both sides of the transition 'divide' to remember that the learning flows both ways: primary and secondary teachers have a lot to learn from each other when it comes to pedagogy and practice.

Moving away from cross-phase partnerships and focusing solely on secondary schools, the most important message for secondary leaders when looking to improve their Key Stage 3 curriculum - and by so doing, academic achievement in Years 7, 8 and 9 - is that Key Stage 3 is a springboard to GCSE success. As such, it must not be regarded as a poor relation to Key Stage 4 for this will only prove to be a self-fulfilling prophecy.

In practice, this means school leaders - particularly the school timetabler - should avoid the temptation to schedule Key Stages 4 and 5 first then fill in the gaps with Key Stage 3 lessons, thus increasing the chances of Key Stage 3 classes being split between two or more teachers. It also means avoiding timetabling non-specialist, underperforming and/or inexperienced teachers for Key Stage 3 lessons, especially in the core subjects and other EBacc subjects. School leaders should utilise their best teachers because this will pay dividends in later years and avoid having to employ remedial interventions to help pupils catch up for lost time.

As well as ensuring that Key Stage 3 lessons are appropriately staffed, the curriculum needs to strike the right balance between providing pupils with a grounding for GCSE and being different enough to Key Stage 4 to be engaging. In order to make Key Stage 3 stand out as unique, you might consider taking advantage of the freedom it offers by contemplating project-based learning and a focus on developing pupils' metacognition and self-regulation skills, for example by employing cooperative learning activities.

Rest assured I'm not suggesting you ditch the traditional academic curriculum and teach something woolly that results in lots of posters and role play. But I am suggesting that you try to teach the curriculum in a way that's different to GCSE and in a way that helps pupils to become their own teachers, to engage in cooperative learning activities and to take ownership of their studies. And there's no shortage of evidence that this approach works. For example, metacognition and self-regulation are ranked number one in the Sutton Trust/Education Endowment Foundation table of educational effectiveness. And John Hattie, in his book 'Visible Learning' (2009), said that "The biggest effects on student learning occur when teachers become learners of their own teaching, and when students become their own teachers".

In Chapter Six we will take a look at what cooperative learning and metacognition look like in practice at Key Stage 3.

CHAPTER SIX

Cooperative learning

Broadly speaking, classroom learning activities can be either competitive, individualistic, or co-operative.

Competitive learning is where pupils compete with each other for marks to see who the best is.

Individualistic learning is where pupils work more independently of each other and, perhaps, of the teacher.

So what, then, is *cooperative learning..?*

Firstly, what it is not: cooperative learning is not simply synonymous with group work.

Rather, cooperative learning is where pupils are required to work together as they learn and have a vested interest in each other's learning. And it's proven to work...

Cooperative learning is, according to the research, the most effective of the three types of learning in terms of academic performance and classroom climate. What's more, cooperative learning can improve pupils' achievement by at least one grade according to John Hattie's meta-analysis of the evidence.

Put simply, cooperative learning refers to those teaching methods which are structured in such a way as to achieve three characteristics thought to enhance learning. Namely, that:

1. Groups succeed or fail together - in other words, individual pupils are held accountable by their peers and peer pressure is used constructively to motivate pupils to learn.

2. Pupils work interactively - in other words, activities involve peer teaching and intensive pupil-led group discussions.

3. One of the lesson objectives is for pupils to learn as part of a team and to help others learn - in other words, groups become motivated to help the weakest members so that the group as a whole performs better. Pupils have a vested interest in each other's success: they only succeed if they all succeed; if one fails, they all fail.

An integral element of this model of cooperative learning is that pupils are held accountable by their teacher for learning and working effectively as a group and for supporting each other to learn. Therefore, as a consequence, pupils come to learn how to work together and to cooperate with each other.

Metacognition

The term metacognition means 'cognition about cognition' or, more informally, 'thinking about thinking'.

The American developmental psychologist John H. Flavell defined metacognition as knowledge about cognition and control of cognition. For example, a person engages in a process of metacognition if she notices that she is having more trouble learning X than

Y; or if it strikes her that she should double-check Z before accepting it as a fact.

Metacognition also involves thinking about your own processes of cognition such as study skills, memory capabilities, and the ability to monitor your own learning. Metacognition needs to be explicitly taught along with subject content.

Metacognitive knowledge is about your own cognitive processes and your understanding of how to regulate those processes in order to maximize your learning.

Metacognitive knowledge includes:

- Content knowledge (declarative knowledge) – in other words, understanding your own capabilities such as evaluating your own knowledge of a topic.
- Task knowledge (procedural knowledge) – in other words, understanding how you perceive the difficulty of a task.
- Strategic knowledge (conditional knowledge) – in other words, understanding how capable you are of using strategies to learn information.

Metacognition is a general term encompassing the study of memory-monitoring and self-regulation, meta-reasoning, consciousness/awareness and auto-consciousness/self-awareness. These capacities are used to maximise your potential to think and to learn.

In practice, to help pupils develop metacognition, we need to give them time to foster understanding and time to reflect on their learning. Reflection might involve pupils rethinking their grasp of important ideas, perhaps with the teacher's guidance. It might involve pupils improving their work through revision based on self-assessment and feedback. It might involve pupils reflecting on their learning and performance.

A linear path through the curriculum content (i.e. teaching it once then moving on) is a mistake. After all, how can pupils master complex ideas and tasks if they encounter them only once? Therefore, the flow of learning must be iterative, pupils must be made fully aware of the need to rethink and revise in light of current learning, and the work must follow the trail back to the original big idea and learning goal.

Let's take an example... In a Key Stage 3 humanities lesson pupils might explore the big question 'What is democracy?' by discussing their experiences and by reading various texts about democracy. Pupils might then develop a theory of democracy and create a concept map for the topic. The teacher might then cause them to rethink their initial ideas by raising a second big question, using an appropriate example: 'What is representative democracy and majority rule - and how does it work?' The pupils might then modify their concept of democracy as they come to understand that democracy can sometimes feel disenfranchising and unfair if the majority of voters do not share your own beliefs and values and if your own MP votes against their constituents' wishes.

As illustrated in this example, in-built rethinking and reflection is a critical and deliberate element of metacognition and self-regulation; moreover, it's central to learning for understanding. We must, therefore, ensure our Key Stage 3 lessons provide opportunities for pupils to constantly reconsider their earlier understandings of the big ideas we've taught them if they are ever to get beyond simplistic thinking and to the heart of the kind of deep understanding that's now required in Key Stage 4 and beyond. Talking of 'beyond'...

The most successful people in life have the capacity to self-monitor and self-adjust as needed. They proactively consider what is working, what isn't, and what might be done better. Another aspect of reflection, therefore, is self-assessment. Here, it is worth considering how pupils will engage in some form of self-evaluation (in order to identify any remaining questions and to set future targets), and how pupils will be helped to take stock of what they have learned and what needs further inquiry or refinement.

Pupils need to be afforded opportunities to self-monitor, self-assess, and self-adjust their work, individually and collectively, as the work progresses. Central to this kind of self-understanding is an honest self-assessment, based on increasing clarity about what we do understand and what we don't; what we have accomplished and what remains to be done.

Crucially, the kind of internal dialogue that's critical to metacognition needs to be explicitly taught; it's not innate. When we look at the 'conditions for learning' in a moment I will explore some practical ways in which we can teach metacognition.

Enquiry-based learning

Both cooperative learning and metacognition involve planning for effective collaborative learning. This means the explicit teaching of communication skills, as well as thinking and reasoning skills.

One possible model for delivering this in the classroom is to get pupils engaging in a project every half-term which is allocated one lesson per week on the timetable. The project might alternate between an individual and a group task. It might be organised on themes allowing a certain degree of autonomy over its content and format.

Where enquiry-based learning of this nature is used, it is important that projects inspire and challenge pupils, are predicated on the idea of every pupil succeeding, and involve genuine research. It is also important that projects have in-built flexibility to allow for a range of abilities, are broken into clear components, and make clear what is expected of each pupil at each stage of their development, thus spelling out the qualities and dimensions on which the work will eventually be judged. Teachers need to foster a sense of whole-class pride in the quality of learning and ensure that, once finished, project work is made public – providing a genuine audience. Project assessments should be used as the primary context for sharing knowledge and skills and this means teaching pupils how to give constructive feedback - another important skill they will need for GCSE and beyond. Finally, teachers need to instil in their pupils the belief that quality means rethinking, reworking, and polishing so that they feel celebrated, not ridiculed, for going back to the drawing board.

Pupils might also be allowed to choose their own talk partners and small groups at the start of Year 7 then their teachers might choose the groups later in the year. Conflicts might be resolved through the use of restorative justice.

There might be a focus on communication skills throughout the year. Ground rules for group talk might be co-constructed with pupils then displayed in the classroom and regularly revisited.

Pupils may complete reflective learning journals once a fortnight that focus on how they learn and what barriers they face, and how they can overcome them.

Whatever approach is taken, Key Stage 3 is an ideal time to think creatively about the timetable and about finding ways of challenging and engaging pupils in ways that will help them grow as learners and develop the skills - as well as the knowledge - they will need at GCSE and beyond.

One particular skill they will need - and, I would argue, one key aspect of metacognition and self-regulation - is transfer, the ability to transfer what has been learnt in one context to other contexts. Perkins & Salomon (1989) identified two mechanisms through which the transfer of knowledge and skills could take place: Low road transfer (in which a skill is practised to near automaticity); and high road transfer (in which transfer relies on the deliberate mindful abstraction of an underlying principle). Pintrich & de Groot (1990), meanwhile, identified the importance of motivation in transfer ('children need the will as well as the skill').

The importance of self-regulation in promoting such transfer became increasingly recognised at the turn of the century (eg Schunk & Ertmer 2000) while Watkins (2001) defined effective transfer as requiring 1. Requisite skills, 2. Choosing to use the skills, 3. Recognising when a particular skill is appropriate in new situations, and 4. Metacognitive awareness, monitoring and checking progress. In short, using Key Stage 3 to help pupils develop the ability to self-regulate will help them to transfer their learning at later stages of their education, thus making their learning universal and therefore meaningful. In other words, it will provide them with the springboard to success at GCSE and beyond.

CHAPTER SEVEN

The conditions for learning

Occasionally, on my teacher-training courses and when the mood takes me, I ask colleagues to draw a picture of something familiar, something a child might doodle. A boat. A lighthouse. A car. An island. A house.

I give them five minutes and ask them to work alone and in silence.

When the five minutes are up, I ask them to swap their drawings with the person next to them so they can peer-assess their artwork. And at this point I share the assessment criteria.

If I'd asked colleagues to draw a house, say, I might at this stage inform them that if they've included a front door they can have five points. If they've drawn a path leading up to that front door, they can be awarded a further five points. If they have five or more windows, each with curtains, they can add another five marks to their tally. A chimney with two chimney pots gets them another five; a garage, five points; a driveway with a car parked on it, five points; and so on.

Delegates then calculate their partner's total score and equate this to a grade before handing it back. It's rare for anyone to get an A or a B. More often than not, colleagues get a D or an E.

Although, by the time they've finished sharing their grades with the class, colleagues have already begun to discern one moral of the story - that we must share the assessment criteria with pupils *before* we set an assignment and we must only assess work using the criteria we make explicit beforehand - I move on from the task without further comment in order to let this realisation (or consolidation of prior knowledge) ruminate.

Next I ask delegates to think of something they're good at and to think about how they became good at it. I then ask them how they know they are good at it - on what evidence is this judgment based?

I ask delegates to think of something they're not very good at and to consider why - what went wrong when they were trying to learn this thing and who, if anyone, was to blame? I then ask them to think about something they are good at now but didn't initially want to learn. What kept them going in lieu of motivation?

Finally, I ask colleagues to think of a time they've helped someone - ideally not a pupil in a school setting, but perhaps a friend or family member - to learn something. To what extent, I ask them, did they understand the subject better once they'd taught it to someone else? And did assessing that person's learning help them to understand the subject even more deeply?

I then canvass colleagues' responses and our subsequent discussions almost always result in the following conclusions:

We decide that most people become good at things through practice, by learning from their mistakes, and by experimenting. People learn best when they engage in a process of trial and error and when they repeat their actions several times, making incremental improvements each time. As the Danish nuclear physicist Niels Bohr once said, "[An expert is] someone who has made all the mistakes which it is possible to make in a very narrow field".

My colleagues and I also conclude that most people know they have a right to feel positive about their achievements because of evidence given in the form of feedback, particularly when they receive praise, and also as a result of receiving a reward for doing well. People also know that they can feel positive about their achievements when they are asked to help others achieve the same end-goal and when they are able to see the results of their labours for themselves.

My colleagues and I conclude that, when learning fails, it's usually because the learner didn't engage in a sufficient amount of practice, didn't work hard enough or lacked focus. Perhaps the feedback the learner received was poor or else they did not act upon it, or at any rate did not act upon it in a timely manner. Perhaps the communication between the teacher and the learner was poor.

More often than not, though, learning fails when the learner lacks sufficient motivation, when they simply aren't interested in learning the thing being taught because it's not personally meaningful to them.

So what, I ask my colleagues, in the absence of motivation - when pupils don't have the **want** to learn - keeps pupils going until they succeed?

My colleagues and I usually conclude that it must be the **need** to learn - having a rationale, a necessity to learn, and therefore taking ownership of the learning - that keeps people going and helps them to overcome their lack of motivation to succeed.

My discussions with my teacher-training colleagues also conclude that by teaching something to a third party we learn more about it ourselves because the act of teaching enables us to gain feedback and make better sense of a topic. Teaching is also a form of learning by doing, of learning through practice. The fact we have to teach something to someone else also addresses the *need* to learn it (we have to learn it in order to teach it to someone else, after all) and we confront the *want* to learn all the time we are teaching - or indeed the lack of motivation.

Once we've taught something and we assess our pupils' learning to see if we've been successful, we learn it for ourselves even more deeply because we discover all the mistakes people can make and we discover all the different ways in which pupils can make sense of a topic. In short, we gain lots of feedback about how to teach the topic the next time.

Assessing someone's learning is also another means of learning by doing. And assessing someone else's learning forces us to define and redefine the standards of pupils' achievements.

Piecing all of these discussions together, and reminding my teacher-training colleagues of the initial task whereby they drew a picture of a house without knowing the criteria on which they'd eventually be assessed, I share what I term 'the conditions for learning' - in other words, the state of affairs that must exist in order for our pupils to be able to learn effectively.

There are, to my mind, six conditions which must be in place in our classrooms in order for learning to happen. These are:

1. Intrinsic motivation

2. Purpose
3. Practice
4. Feedback
5. Metacognition
6. Assessment

Let's take a look at each of these six 'conditions for learning' in turn...

1. Intrinsic motivation

In order to create the conditions for pupils to learn, we need to establish their **want** to learn - we need them to be motivated to learn. This involves them understanding *why it matters* that they learn what we intend to teach them.

Intrinsic motivation is the self-desire to seek out new things and new challenges, to gain new knowledge. Often, intrinsic motivation is driven by an inherent interest or enjoyment in the task itself, and exists within the individual rather than relying on external pressures or necessity.

Put simply, it's the desire to do something even though there is no reward except a sense of accomplishment at achieving that thing. Intrinsic motivation is a natural motivational tendency and is a critical element in cognitive, social, and physical development.

Pupils who are intrinsically motivated are more likely to engage in a task willingly as well as work to improve their skills, which will - in turn - increase their capabilities. Pupils are likely to be intrinsically motivated if they:
- attribute their educational results to factors under their own control, also known as *autonomy*
- believe in their own ability to succeed in specific situations or to accomplish a task - also known as a sense of *self-efficacy*

- are genuinely interested in accomplishing something to a high level of proficiency, knowledge and skill, not just in achieving good grades - also known as *mastery*.

2. Purpose

In order to create the right conditions for pupils to learn, we need to establish their **need** to learn - we need them to have clear targets and to know why they need to learn what we intend to teach them and *how they will use* that learning later.

If the *want* to learn is concerned with intrinsic motivation, we might loosely argue that the *need* to learn - the purpose - is linked to extrinsic motivation...

Extrinsic motivation refers to the performance of an activity in order to attain a desired outcome and it is the opposite of intrinsic motivation. Extrinsic motivation comes from influences outside of the individual's control; a rationale, a necessity, a need. Common forms of extrinsic motivation are rewards (for example money or prizes), or - conversely- the threat of punishment.

We can provide pupils with a rationale for learning by sharing the 'big picture' with them. In other words, we can continually explain how their learning fits in to the module, the course, the qualification, their careers and to success in work and life. For example, we can explain how today's lesson connects with yesterday's lesson and how the learning will be extended or consolidated next lesson, as well as how it will be assessed at a later stage. We can explain how this learning will become useful in later life, too. And we can connect the learning in one subject with the learning in other subjects, making explicit the transferability of knowledge and skills and the interconnectedness of skills in everyday life.

This is not to suggest that pupils will possess *either* intrinsic *or* extrinsic motivation. Rather, it is desirable for pupils to possess or develop both. Pupils should both *want* and *need* to learn. However, it is natural that some pupils will lack the want to learn and so instilling in them the need to learn becomes all the more important.

However, a word of warning: the need to learn should be about explaining the rationale, outlining why acquiring the knowledge and skills you're teaching will be useful to pupils now and in the future, and it should be about showing pupils the big picture, connecting the learning. It should not be about using a carrot and a stick - rewards and sanctions - to motivate pupils because social psychological research has indicated that the use of extrinsic rewards has the potential to reduce the level of pupils' intrinsic motivation. In one study demonstrating this effect, for example, children who expected to be (and were indeed) rewarded with a ribbon and a gold star for drawing pictures spent less time playing with the drawing materials in subsequent observations than children who were assigned to an unexpected reward condition.

Having said this, the nature of the reward matters. For example, in another study pupils who were rewarded with a book demonstrated better reading behaviours in the future, implying that some rewards do not undermine intrinsic motivation and can be educationally beneficial.

In the **bonus chapter** on project-based learning I will explain how to ensure a project has purpose. For example, I will explain that a project can fulfil an educational purpose if it provides opportunities to build metacognition and character skills such as collaboration, communication, and critical thinking, which will serve pupils well in the workplace as in life. A project can also fulfil an educational purpose if pupils conduct a real-life inquiry, rather than finding information in textbooks or on the Internet then making a poster. A project can also fulfil an educational purpose if it makes learning meaningful by emphasising the need to create high-quality products and performances through the formal use of feedback and drafting. And finally, a project can fulfil an educational purpose if it ends with a product being presented to a real audience.

But as well being educationally meaningful, we need to make sure work is made personally meaningful. A project can be given a personal purpose if we begin by triggering pupils' curiosity. In other words, at the start of the first lesson on the project, we use a 'hook' to engage our pupils' interest and initiate questioning. A project can also be made personally meaningful to pupils if we pose a big question which captures the heart of the project in clear, compelling language, and which gives pupils a sense of purpose and challenge. And finally, a project can be made personally meaningful to pupils if they are given some choice about how to conduct the project and present their findings.

3. Practice

In order to create the conditions for pupils to learn, we need to ensure they are afforded opportunities to **learn by doing**, and to learn from their mistakes (what we call 'the open loop').

In Chapter Eight on homework, I will explore the importance of practice tasks in more detail. I will, for example, explain how practice builds proficiency and mastery. I will also share three forms of practice, namely:

1. *Spaced repetition.* This is where information is learnt initially then repeated again several times at increasingly long intervals so that pupils get to the point of almost forgetting what they've learnt and have to delve into their long-term memories to retrieve their prior knowledge, thus strengthening those memories.

2. Retrieval practice. This is testing or quizzing (such as multiple choice) used not for the purposes of assessment but for reinforcement and to provide pupils with feedback information on what they know and don't yet know so that they can better focus their future studies.

3. Cognitive disfluency (otherwise known as desirable difficulties). This is a memory technique that makes learning 'stick' by placing artificial barriers in the way of pupils' initial learning. Doing this means that the process of encoding (learning something for the first time) is made harder so that the process of retrieval (recalling that learning later, say in a test) is made quicker and easier.

The power of practice - of learning by doing through a process of trial and error - has a foundation in neurochemistry...

Whenever we do something – think, move, read this book – our brain sends a signal (like an electric charge) along the neurones in our brains and through our nerve fibres to our muscles. In other words, every skill we possess – swinging a golf club, writing great fiction, playing the piano – is created by chains of nerve fibres carrying small electrical impulses like the signals travelling through a circuit. Each time we practise something, a different highly specific circuit is illuminated in our heads and it is these circuits that control our thoughts and movements. Indeed, the circuit *is* the movement because it dictates the content of each thought and the timing and strength of each muscle contraction.

More importantly, each time we practise something – be it a mental or physical skill – our nerve fibres are coated in a layer of insulating material called *myelin* which acts in much the same way as the rubber insulation that coats a copper wire: it makes the electrical impulses stronger and faster by preventing the signals from leaking out.

Each time we practise a skill, a new layer of myelin is added to the neurone and the thicker the myelin gets, the better it insulates our nerve fibres and, therefore, the faster our movements and thoughts become. But that's not all. As well as getter faster, our thoughts and movements also become more accurate as we add more and more layers of myelin. Why should this be? Because myelin regulates the velocity with which those electrical impulses travel through our nerve fibres, speeding up or slowing down the signals so that they hit our synapses at exactly the right moment. And timing is all important because neurones are binary: either they fire or they don't. Whether or not they fire is dependent on whether the incoming impulse is big enough to exceed their so-called "threshold of activation".

Neurochemistry teaches us, therefore, that every skill can be improved and perfected by performing it repeatedly because this helps us to hone our neural circuitry. But not all forms of practice are equal. We create myelin most effectively when we engage in *deliberate practice*

Deliberate practice is about struggling in certain targeted ways – placing artificial barriers in the way of our success in order to make it harder to learn something. In other words, you slow your learning down and force yourself to make mistakes. This is what Robert Bjork calls "desirable difficulties" and I will explore this concept in Chapter Eight on homework. For now, suffice to say, the act of slowing down and making mistakes ensures we are operating at the edges of our ability. So the best form of practice – and therefore the best way to create more myelin – is to set yourself a target just beyond your current ability but within your reach. This is what Lev Vygotsky calls the "zone of proximal development" and what Robert Bjork calls "the sweet spot". This spot is the "optimal gap between what [we] know and what [we're] trying to do [and] when [we] find that sweet spot, learning takes off".

In the **bonus chapter** on the habits of academic success, I will explore what all the high-achieving pupils I've ever taught had in common. Having studied their methods and interviewed them, I have discovered that it is a case of cause and effect: it is precisely because these pupils attended school, were well-organised, completed work on time, and had an end goal in mind that they achieved excellent grades in their final exams. In short, the cause was diligent study and determination; the effect was high achievement.

In that chapter I will also argue that one way to emulate the success of my best pupils is to acquire a toolkit of effective study skills such as:

Self-quizzing - this is about retrieving knowledge and skills from memory and is far more effective than simply re-reading a text.

Elaboration - this is about relating new material to what pupils already know, explaining it to somebody else, or explaining how it relates to the wider world.

Generation - this is when pupils attempt to answer a question or solve a problem before being shown the answer or the solution.

Reflection - this involves taking a moment to review what has been learned by asking questions such as: What went well? What could have gone better? What other knowledge or experience does it remind me of? What strategies could I use next time to get better results?

Calibration - this is about removing the illusion of knowing and pupils actually answering all the questions or testing themselves on all the subject content even if they think they know the answers and that it is too easy.

4. Feedback

In order to create the conditions for pupils to learn, we need to ensure they receive - and produce - information about what they have mastered and what they still need to practice.

Feedback should redirect the pupil's and the teacher's actions to help the pupil achieve their target. Effective feedback: addresses faulty interpretations; comments on rather than grades work; provides cues or prompts for further work; is timely, specific and clear; and is focused on task and process rather than on praising.

Feedback works best when it is explicit about the marking criteria, offers suggestions for improvement, and is focused on how pupils can close the gap between their current and their desired performance; it does not focus on presentation or quantity of work.

Feedback can promote the growth mindset if it: is as specific as possible; focuses on factors within pupils' control; focuses on factors which are dependent on effort not ability; and motivates rather than frustrates pupils.

Self- and peer-assessment can prove effective strategies - particularly as we want our pupils to become increasingly metacognitive in their approach to learning - because they: give pupils greater responsibility for their learning; allow pupils to help and be helped by each other; encourage collaboration and reflection; enable pupils to see their progress; and help pupils to see for themselves how to improve.

But self- and peer-assessment needs to be used wisely and pupils need to be helped to develop the necessary skills and knowledge because research suggests eighty per cent of the feedback pupils give each other is wrong. However, it is worth investing time in helping pupils to improve their self-assessment skills because research suggests it increases pupils' achievement.

Ultimately, though, the only useful feedback is that which is acted upon – it is crucial, therefore, that the teacher knows the pupil and knows when and what kind of feedback to give, then plans time for pupils to act on the feedback they receive. For example, DIRT - 'directed improvement and reflection time' - is a great use of lesson time at Key Stage 3 and helps to condition pupils in the drafting and re-drafting process, as well as gets them used to responding positively to feedback, to learning from their mistakes, and to improving through a process of trial and error.

5. Metacognition

In order to create the conditions for pupils to learn, we need to ensure that they are afforded opportunities to explain key concepts to each other and **learn by teaching**, thereby taking ownership of their own and each other's learning. I've already written in some detail about metacognition and cooperative learning so shall not do so again here, except to share a few practical ideas for teaching metacognition.

Above, I explained that the most successful people in life have the capacity to self-monitor and self-adjust as needed; they proactively consider what is working, what isn't, and what might be done better. In order to prepare our pupils for Key Stage 4 and beyond, therefore, we need to engage them in some form of self-evaluation, teaching them how to take stock of what they have learned and what needs further inquiry or refinement.

In practice, this means that pupils need opportunities in lessons to self-monitor, self-assess, and self-adjust their work, individually and collectively, as the work progresses. We can do this by:

- Allocating five minutes in the middle and at the end of a lesson in order to consider 'What have we found out? What remains unresolved or unanswered?

- Asking pupils to attach a self-assessment form to every formal piece of work they hand in
- Including a one-minute essay at the end of an instruction-based lesson in which pupils summarise the two or three main points and the questions that still remain for them (and, thus, next time, for the teacher)
- Asking pupils to attach a note to any formal piece of work in which they are honest about what they do and do not understand
- Teaching pupils to evaluate work in the same way that teachers do so that pupils become more accurate as peer reviewers and self-assessors, and more inclined to "think like teachers" in their work.
- Starting lessons with a survey of the most burning questions pupils may have. Then, as part of the final plenary, judge how well the questions were addressed, which ones remain, and what new ones emerged.
- Leaving the second half of a unit deliberately 'open' to allow pupils to frame and pursue the inquiry (rather than be directed by the teacher) based on the key questions that remain and clues that emerge at the end of the first half
- Getting pupils to develop a self-profile of their strengths and weaknesses as learners at the start of the year whereby they consider how they learn best, what strategies work well for them, what type of learning is most difficult, and what they wish to improve upon. Then, structure periodic opportunities for pupils to monitor their efforts and reflect on their struggles, and successes, and possible edits to their own profiles.

(This list is adapted from **Teach 2: Educated Risks** *by M J Bromley 2016)*

6. Assessment

Finally, in order to create the conditions for pupils to learn, we need to involve them in making judgments about their own and others' achievements against the learning outcomes.

There's a whole chapter on assessment later in this book so I won't dedicate too much time to it here but I do want to explore a couple of methods of assessing pupils' understanding:

First, let's consider **questioning**...

Questioning - and indeed all forms of classroom discussion - is a great way to assess pupils' understanding and, more importantly, of deepening that understanding.

Questions make pupils smarter because they make pupils think. Questions should only be used if they cause thinking and/or provide information for the teacher about what to do next. The best model of questioning is ABC whereby questions are passed around the classroom and pupils agree/disagree with, build upon, and challenge each other's responses. The Japanese call this *neriage* which means 'to polish' – pupils polish each other's answers, refining them, challenging each other's thinking.

It's a well-known fact by now that increasing 'wait time' – the amount of time the teacher waits for an answer to their question before either answering it themselves or asking someone else – makes pupils' answers longer, more confident, and increases pupils' ability to respond.

In open questions, the rubric defines the rigour. In multiple choice questions the options define the rigour. Effective assessment combines open and multiple-choice questions.

Second, let's take a look at **constructive alignment**...

Constructive alignment is another great assessment tool. It's a concept that derives from cognitive psychology and constructivist theory and recognises the importance of linking new material to experiences in the learner's memory, as well as extrapolating that material to possible future contexts – connecting the learning, showing the bigger picture. The teacher makes a deliberate alignment between the planned learning activities and the learning outcomes. This is a conscious effort to provide the learner with a clearly defined goal, and a well-designed learning activity that is appropriate for the task. But, more importantly for our present purposes, it provides the pupil with well-designed assessment criteria for giving feedback once they've completed that task. In constructive alignment the teacher starts with the outcomes they want pupils to learn, and then aligns teaching and assessment to those outcomes.

Constructive alignment marries well with the SOLO (structure of observed learning outcomes) taxonomy and helps to map levels of understanding that can be built into intended learning outcomes and create assessment criteria or rubrics.

SOLO consists of five levels of understanding:

1. *Pre-structural*: a pupil hasn't understood the point and offers a simple – incorrect – response;

2. *Uni-structural*: a pupil's response only focuses on one relevant aspect;

3. *Multi-structural:* here, a pupil's response focuses on several relevant aspects but these are treated independently of each other;

4. *Relational*: here, the different aspects seen at the multi-structural level have become integrated to form a coherent whole;

5. *Extended abstract*: the integrated whole is now conceptualised at a higher level of abstraction.

As pupils move up the five levels, their understanding grows from surface to deep to conceptual.

The SOLO taxonomy also helps develop a growth mindset because pupils come to understand that declarative and functioning learning outcomes are the result of effort and the use of effective strategies rather than the result of innate ability.

*

Once all six of these conditions for learning are in place, pupils will not only be able to learn but will be able to transfer their learning from one context to another - the measure of true learning.

To further support our pupils in developing this ability to 'transfer' their learning, we should also: Allow a sufficient amount of time for initial learning to take place; plan for distributed – or spaced – learning and engage in deliberate practice; make sure pupils are motivated to learn by planning work with sufficient challenge; teach information in multiple, contrasting contexts and/or in abstract form; teach metacognition so that pupils become expert at monitoring and regulating their learning.

*

The five keys to lesson planning

Now that we've established and defined the six conditions for learning, let's take a look at how we might incorporate these into our planning...

Lessons which meet the six conditions for learning which I outline above possess five common elements of design - what we might call a 'design for learning' or the 'five keys to lesson planning':

Firstly, lessons that meet the six conditions for learning make explicit the big picture. They do this by connecting the learning in three ways: 1. They articulate a clear learning goal that pupils understand - in other words, pupils are told where the lesson is headed. 2. They articulate a clear purpose for the learning - in other words, pupils are told why the learning goal is important and why they are learning what they're learning. 3. They ensure that pupils' starting points (what they already know as well as their misconceptions) are identified through pre-tests.

Secondly, lessons that meet the six conditions for learning ensure that subject content is tailored to meet individual needs and to match individual skills, interests, and styles. We do this by personalising the learning, by using diagnostic data about pupils' starting points and misconceptions (both that gathered from pre-tests and that gleaned from ongoing formative assessments in class) in order to inform the lesson planning process.

Thirdly, lessons that meet the six conditions for learning ensure that the learning activities pique and maintain pupils' interest by grabbing their attention from the very beginning. They do this by using sensory 'hooks' and by ensuring that the lesson is appropriately paced, and that subject content is appropriately varied and challenging.

Fourthly, lessons that meet the six conditions for learning ensure that pupils acquire the necessary experiences, knowledge and skills to meet the learning goals but in so doing they remember that less is more: they cover a smaller amount of curriculum content so that they can explore each concept in greater depth and detail - and from a range of different perspectives - than they would be able to achieve if they attempted to 'get through' more content.

Finally, lessons that meet the six conditions for learning provide pupils with regular opportunities to reflect on their progress, to revise their thinking and to re-draft their work, acting on the formative feedback they receive from teacher-, peer- and self-assessments.

And those are the five keys to lesson planning that will unlock the six conditions for learning I outlined earlier.

Here are a few other tips for planning Key Stage 3 lessons with which to conclude this section on the curriculum:

- When planning lessons, we should focus on what pupils will be made to think about rather than on what they will do. We might, for example, organise a lesson around a big question.
- We need to repeat learning several times – at least three times, in fact – if it is to penetrate pupils' long-term memories.
- Tests interrupt forgetting and reveal what has actually been learnt as well as what gaps exist. Accordingly, we should run pre-tests at the start of every unit – perhaps as a multiple choice quiz – which will provide cues and improve subsequent learning. Retrieval activities like this also help pupils prepare for exams.
- We should plan lessons so that the information we teach 'sticks' in pupils' memories. We can do this by:
  o ensuring that each lesson clearly articulates and is built around a simple idea – i.e. being clear about the key take-away message from each lesson, which could be a question or hypothesis.
  o using metaphor to relate new ideas to prior knowledge and to create images in pupils' minds.
  o piquing pupils' curiosity before we fill gaps in pupils' knowledge (thus convincing pupils they need the information we're about to give them access to). This can be done by asking pupils to make predictions or by

setting a hypothesis to be proven or disproven.

o making abstract ideas concrete by grounding them in sensory reality (i.e. making pupils feel something). The richer – sensorily and emotionally – new information is, the more strongly it is encoded in pupils' memories.

o making ideas credible - showing rather than telling pupils something (e.g. experiments, field studies, etc. beat textbooks for 'stickability').

*

In Chapter Eight we will examine ways of making Key Stage 3 homework more engaging and meaningful but first, in a **bonus chapter** exclusive to this edition of the book, let's explore project-based learning in greater depth...

BONUS CHAPTER

What motivates pupils?

We know from Ron Berger's book *An Ethic of Excellence* that the first step towards encouraging pupils to produce high-quality work is to set assessment tasks which inspire and challenge them and which are predicated on the idea that every pupil will succeed, not just finish the task but produce work which represents personal excellence. We also know that the most effective assessment tasks offer pupils an opportunity to engage in genuine research not just research invented for the classroom. We know, too, that a pupil's finished product needs a real audience and that the role of the teacher is to help pupils to get their work ready for the public eye. This means there is a genuine reason to do the work well, not just because the teacher wants it that way. Not every piece of work can be of genuine importance, of course, but every piece of work can be displayed, presented, appreciated, and judged.

We know that assessment tasks work best when they are structured in such a way as to make it difficult for pupils to fall too far behind or fail. Tasks also work best when they are broken into a set of clear components so that pupils have to progress through checkpoints to ensure they are keeping up. Good tasks have in-built flexibility to allow for a range of abilities. We also know that assessment tasks work best when they have in-built rubrics, checklists if you like, which make clear what is expected of each pupil at each stage of development. In other words, the rubric spells out exactly what components are required in the assignment, what the timeline for completion is, and on what qualities and dimensions the work will be judged.

However, we know it is not enough simply to make a list, a rubric, of what makes a good finished product, be that an essay or a science experiment. It is not enough to read a great piece of literature and analyse the writing, or to look at the work of a great scientist. If we want our pupils to write a strong essay, to design a strong experiment, we need to show them what a great essay or experiment looks like. We need to admire models, find inspiration in them, and analyse their strengths and weaknesses. In short, we need to work out what makes them strong. And what is the best way of achieving all of the above and, therefore, one means of delivering the five principles of well-planned lessons we explored in the previous chapter? According to Berger - and many others besides - the answer is project-based learning.

*

When I think back to my own school days, the most lasting and colourful memories I have - well, the second most lasting and colourful memories I have (because what happens behind the bike sheds stays behind the bike sheds) - are of project work. I recall the excitement of being given a brief and knowing that I had the freedom to meet that brief in any way I wanted, to work independently over the course of several lessons, gathering evidence and testing a hypothesis or answering a big question, then presenting my findings in a creative and personal way. Many of us, when asked about a positive memory of school, will similarly remember a research project with real-world application that engaged us and that we were able to share with our friends and family.

According to the Galileo Educational Network (2004) - which designs and delivers enquiry-based learning in some American schools - project-based learning is "a dynamic process of being open to wonder and puzzlements and coming to know and understand the world". They go on to say that project-based learning is "a process whereby pupils are actively involved in their learning, formulate questions, investigate far and wide, and build understandings, meanings and knowledge [that is] new to pupils and may be used to answer a question, to develop a solution or to support a position or point of view."

Research, such as that carried out by Kuhne in 1995, suggests that using project-based learning with pupils can help them to become more creative, more positive and more independent. It helps if project-based learning forms part of the whole school culture, if it is common practice across all classes and year groups, and if it is the accepted mode of learning such as is the case in Studio Schools and UTCs, for example...

Studio Schools and UTCs have embraced project-based learning as a means of preparing young people for the world of work. They cite evidence that employers are looking for – and yet not finding – key employability skills amongst school leavers. In a recent CBI Employer Survey, for example, seventy per cent of employers said they wanted to see the government do more to make the employability skills of young people its top education priority. However, extensive research shows that equipping young people with employability skills alone is not enough. In a competitive and uncertain world, young people also need to think creatively, build resilience, and be able to respond effectively to rapidly changing circumstances. The evidence suggests that embedding creativity and an ability to respond successfully to change is vital if the UK is to compete in an increasingly globalised service economy. The question for schools has been 'how'?

Studio Schools took their name from the Renaissance period (1400-1700) when working and learning were integrated. Pupils were taught by an experienced master – such as Leonardo da Vinci, Raphael, and Michelangelo – in the same workshop in which the master created and produced his work. Their goal is to take this tradition and apply it to the 21st Century by creating schools in which pupils study academic and vocational subjects by means of real work experience, such as happens in medicine and law. There is strong evidence that, by bringing working and learning together, pupils can perform better, and be better prepared for their working lives. Project-based learning lies at the heart of these schools' curricula. Pupils learn through enterprise projects based in school, in local businesses, and in their surrounding communities.

In order for other schools to make project-based learning a part of their culture, too, senior leaders must have a clearly articulated vision for developing it and they must be strong in dedicating time and money to it, even in spite of competing pressures. In its early stages, there needs to be a group of enthusiastic champions willing to try it out and promote the advantages. Teachers need to collaborate and support each other. Problem-solving and investigative skills also need to be valued throughout the school.

But, whilst a whole school commitment to project-based learning is desirable, it is by no means essential... individual teachers can make it work in beautiful isolation in their own classrooms... According to Drayton and Falk (2002), individual classrooms in which teachers emphasise project-based learning - even when the rest of the school does not - tend to have the following characteristics:

- Projects take the form of real-life problems and work within the context of the curriculum and/or local community.
- Projects capitalise on the areas of pupils' natural curiosity.
- Data and information are actively used, interpreted, refined, digested and discussed.
- Teachers, pupils and other key staff (including, say, the school librarian) work together to plan projects.
- The local community is connected with the project in some way, either as research material or audience, or indeed both.
- The teacher continually models the behaviours required of the pupil-researchers.
- The teacher uses the language required of the pupil-researchers on an ongoing basis.
- Pupils take ownership of their own learning from beginning to end.
- The teacher facilitates the process of gathering and presenting information.
- The teacher and pupils use technology to advance their project, both in information gathering and presenting.
- The teacher embraces project-based learning as both curriculum content and pedagogy.
- The teacher and pupils interact more frequently and more actively than during traditional instruction.

Building a culture of project-based learning in your classroom also means recognising, supporting and teaching the role of metacognition. Certainly, project-based learning provides opportunities for pupils to develop life skills (as explained by Hacker (1999) and Huhlthau (1988) among others) such as character or grit.

*

There are three strands of project-based learning well worth remembering - indeed, in many ways, these three are the cornerstones of effective projects:

1. A genuine outcome
2. Multiple drafts
3. Ongoing assessment

1. A genuine outcome

If pupils are to commit time and effort to their project, they need to know that there is a genuine outcome, a real audience and means of exhibition for their work. In other words, if pupils know their work is going to be put on public display, there to be critiqued by members of the public, including their family and friends and not just their teachers, they are more likely to work hard and produce their best quality work.

2. Multiple drafts

In real life, when the quality of work matters, we rarely submit our first attempt at something. By the time this book is published, for example, I will have drafted and redrafted it several times (so just imagine how bad my first draft must have been!) But in many schools pupils hand in their first attempt at something, have it marked and returned, then discard it before moving on to the next task.

Project-based learning enables pupils to positively engage with the drafting and redrafting process, and encourages them to make time for and recognise the importance of polishing work until such a time as it represents their very best efforts. Producing multiple drafts is not only a great way of teaching pupils about the real life importance of redrafting, but it also provides great opportunities for personalised assessment... talking of which...

3. Ongoing assessment

Producing multiple drafts helps pupils to engage in formative assessment, learning from feedback and making gradual improvements. Re-drafting also enables pupils to learn from each other by critiquing each other's work. Regarded in this way, critique, - far from being a distraction or added burden - becomes integral to the learning process. Critique can become a lesson in its own right, providing opportunities for the teacher to give instruction, to introduce or refine concepts and skills. Such lessons can also bring pupils' misunderstandings to the fore, enabling the class to respond en masse.

Ron Berger argues that effective feedback is kind, specific and helpful. This is also a good way to structure critique sessions:

Kind: Presenting their work for critique puts pupils in a vulnerable position. The person critiquing work, on the other hand, can - in their enthusiasm and eagerness to help - say hurtful things, albeit inadvertently. Therefore, pupils need to be taught how to be kind and avoid personal attacks.

Specific: Although it is important to be kind, feedback must not - as a result - become too vague and anodyne; it must offer specific advice about how to improve if it is to be useful.

Helpful: Critique should not just be about articulating what is strong and what is not; it should also be about working out how to make the work even better; it should offer suggestions and ideas.

There are two main types of critique session: instructional critique and peer critique.

1. An **instructional critique** session is led by the teacher and usually involves the entire class. It can be used to introduce a model at the start of a project.

2. A ***peer critique*** session is what pupils use in order to get feedback on their drafts. Peer critique sessions are usually carried out in pairs or small groups, though they can also be carried out by a full class.

They might take the form of '**gallery**' critique whereby work is displayed on the walls around the classroom and the class walks around the room taking notes on the drafts and sticking post-it notes to them offering general impressions and suggestions.

They might take the form of '**dilemma**' critique whereby pupils are placed in groups of four or five and share something they're struggling with on their product, or share a draft, and then allow their fellow pupils to discuss possible solutions.

They might take the form of '**workshop**' critique whereby pupils are placed in groups of three with specific teacher-generated questions about the product in hand. Pupils take turns presenting their product to the other two pupils and then discuss the questions as a way to improve the product's quality. Each pupil spends about 10–15 minutes on presenting and receiving feedback/critique.

Finally, they might take the form of '**pair**' critique whereby two pupils work together to provide deeper critique, really digging into a product, evaluating the work, and challenging each other for 15–20 minutes.

*

Project-based learning also works best when pupils regard the project as personally meaningful and when it fulfils an educational purpose - in other words, when it is an integral part of the curriculum.

Ensuring a project is meaningful

A project can be made personally meaningful if we begin by triggering pupils' curiosity. In other words, at the start of the first lesson on the project, we use a 'hook' to engage our pupils' interest and initiate questioning. A hook can be anything: a video, a lively discussion, a guest speaker, a field trip, or a text. Many pupils find schoolwork meaningless because they don't perceive a need to know what they're being taught. They are not motivated by their teacher's insistence that they should learn something because they'll need it later in life or for the next module on the course, or because it might be in the exam. With a compelling project, however, the reason for the learning becomes clear: pupils need to know this in order to meet the challenge they've just accepted.

A project can also be made personally meaningful to pupils if we pose a big question which captures the heart of the project in clear, compelling language, and which gives pupils a sense of purpose and challenge. A big question should be provocative, open, and complex. The question can be abstract or concrete; or it can be focused on solving a problem. Without a big question, pupils may not understand why they are undertaking a project. They may know that the series of activities they are engaged in are in some way connected but may not be clear as to how or why. The big question is the string that binds the project together.

A project can be made personally meaningful to pupils if they are given some choice about how to conduct the project and present their findings. Indeed, the more choice, the better. Where choice is limited, pupils can select what topic to study within a general big question or choose how to design, create, and present their findings. In the middle of the choice spectrum, we might provide a small menu of options for creative final 'products' in order to prevent pupils from becoming overwhelmed by too many choices. Where choice is broad, pupils can decide what 'products' they will create, what resources they will use, and how they will use their time. Pupils might also choose their project's topic and big question.

Ensuring a project fulfils an educational purpose

A project can fulfil an educational purpose if it provides opportunities to build metacognition and character skills such as collaboration, communication, and critical thinking, which will serve pupils well in the workplace as in life.

A project can also fulfil an educational purpose if pupils conduct a real-life inquiry, rather than finding information in textbooks or on the Internet then making a poster. In projects with real-life application, pupils follow a trail that begins with their own questions, leads to a search for resources and the discovery of answers, and often ultimately leads to generating new questions, testing ideas, and drawing their own conclusions. With real-life projects comes innovation—a new answer to a big question, a new product, or an individually generated solution to a problem.

A project can also fulfil an educational purpose if it makes learning meaningful by emphasising the need to create high-quality products and performances through the formal use of feedback and drafting. As part of project-based learning, pupils learn that most people's first attempts don't result in high quality. Instead, frequent revision is a feature of real-world work. In addition to providing direct feedback, we can coach pupils in using rubrics and other sets of assessment criteria in order for pupils to critique each other's work.

Finally, a project can fulfil an educational purpose if it ends with a product being presented to a real audience. Work is more meaningful when it is produced not only for the teacher or the test but for a real public audience. This makes pupils care more about the quality of their work.

Let's take a look at how to plan, run and assess a project...

Planning a project

When planning a project, it is crucial that the topic is worthy of pupils' time and effort and will retain their interest over the medium-term. It is also important that it will deliver sufficient curriculum content to be worthy of its timetabled commitment.

When selecting a topic, we should begin with the syllabus's programmes of study and select an area that will intrigue and interest pupils. The next step is to set out objectives for the project and to plan the activities. We should choose a curriculum-based theme for which background knowledge will already have been developed prior to the project starting because pupils will need to bring a strong background of experience and knowledge with them. We should consider whether or not the theme presents sufficient opportunities to engage all pupils in the class, including males and females, the highly motivated as well as those who require a lot of encouragement, and the more able as well as those who require more support and scaffolding.

If using project-based learning for the first time, we should try to limit the scope of the project in terms of time, topic and end-product, and focus on ensuring the success of all pupils. We should consider how many product formats we are willing to teach and make sure that pupils share information in a way that is very simple or very familiar to them.

Running a project

As well as a means of delivering the curriculum, projects help pupils to acquire and develop research and employability skills. This works best when project-based learning is integrated within the curriculum, is taught with a focus on developing critical thinkers, is made relevant to pupils' lives and needs, and is related to their past experiences.

As pupils work through the project, we teachers - by employing a personalised approach - need to help our pupils to locate, analyse and use the information they find. We need to assist them to clarify their thinking through questioning, paraphrasing and talking through tasks. We need to provide them with opportunities to record information, and we need to evaluate their progress.

Broadly speaking, there are five main phases to a project:

Phase 1: Piquing curiosity and agreeing key questions for investigation

Project-based learning begins by piquing pupils' interest in or curiosity about a topic. It is a big question that begs an answer, a hypothesis that demands to be proven or disproven, a puzzle that simply must be solved.

For those pupils with little or no background knowledge of a topic, we need to provide information and contextual knowledge in order to motivate pupils. Once pupils are interested and engaged in a general topic or theme, they need to be involved in determining what particular questions will be investigated, how they might find the information they need about a particular topic, how to present information to a particular audience, and what criteria for evaluating their research product and process might best be used.

Phase 2: Assimilating existing knowledge and gathering new evidence

Next, pupils need to think about the information they already have on the topic and agree the information they need to find and how best to gather that information. Pupils may need to spend a considerable amount of time exploring and analysing the information they have and they gather in order to determine their key focus for the project.

We will often need to help pupils understand that the information they find, whether in a book, a newspaper or on the internet, was created by people with particular beliefs and purposes and that, therefore, the information is likely to be subjective rather than objective. As such, it's important that we teach pupils to be able to identify emotive language and bias.

Phase 3: Finding a focus

Next, pupils will find a focus for their project. A focus is the aspect of a topic that, armed with all the information they need, the pupil decides to investigate. Coming to a focus can be very difficult for pupils because it involves more than just narrowing the scope of the topic. It also involves agreeing a big question or hypothesis, perhaps offering a personal perspective, too.

Phase 4: Organising and sharing information

Pupils then need to organise the information they've gathered, putting the information into their own words and creating a presentation - using their preferred format perhaps.

Once the presentation is ready, it should be shared, ideally with a real audience outside the classroom.

Teaching pupils audience appreciation skills and strategies, focusing on the positive, helps to support pupils through this phase.

Phase 5: Evaluating the project

Finally, when a research project is complete, pupils need to understand and question the assessment criteria, to identify the various steps in their project process, and to share their feelings about that process.

Pupils should be able to articulate the importance of this work in terms of how it has helped them develop their metacognitive skills, and they should be able to see connections between their project work in school and work or activities that they have completed outside of school.

Assessing a project

When designing projects, we need to plan for ongoing assessments and these assessments should take three forms: diagnostic, formative and summative.

1. *Diagnostic assessment* is used to find out which metacognitive skills and strategies pupils already know and can use at the start of a project which can then be built on during the project. Areas of weakness and difficulty can also be targeted at this stage to help plan direct instruction during the project. Diagnostic assessments also help us to recognise when personalised or differentiated instruction may be necessary for certain pupils in a class.

2. *Formative assessment* is critical in the planning of project-based learning activities. Ongoing formative assessment helps us to identify the development of our pupils' skills and strategies and to monitor pupils' planning, retrieving, processing and creating skills during research activity. This ongoing assessment allows us to modify instruction, adapt the project activity and support pupils with special instructional needs.

3. *Summative assessment* is carried out at the end of the project in order to provide information to pupils, parents and teachers about pupils' progress and achievement on the project. This type of assessment helps us and our pupils to plan for further projects. Summative assessment assesses both the content and the process of the project.

Project assessments should involve pupils in identifying and/or creating the criteria used to evaluate pupil work and this criteria should be communicated before pupils begin tasks so that they can plan for success and so that they understand what is expected of them.

Project assessments should form part of an ongoing process rather than be regarded as an isolated event, and should focus on both process and product. Assessments should also provide opportunities for pupils to revise their work, enabling them to set goals and improve their learning by providing a status report on how well pupils can demonstrate their learning and progress at any one time. Assessment feedback should be developmentally appropriate, age-appropriate, and should consider pupils' cultural and individual needs. Assessment data should take into account multiple sources of evidence (including both formal and informal), and provide opportunities for pupils to demonstrate what they know, understand and can do.

*

To conclude this chapter on project-based learning, here is a useful flowchart summarising the process:

1. Pupils select a topic to research within the parameters set by the teacher.

2. Pupils develop and support a position or point of view, this may be a big question that needs answering or a hypothesis that needs proving or disproving.

3. Pupils relate their existing knowledge and understanding of their topic and identify any gaps and areas that require further study.

4. Pupils conduct research in order to develop an in-depth understanding. This may include using textbooks, the Internet, and conducting interviews. Pupils are

taught the relevant research skills as well as codes of ethics and confidentiality as appropriate.

4. Pupils record information using the most appropriate note-taking strategies.

5. Pupils carefully select and evaluate key information from a variety of sources.

6. Pupils create a report or presentation based on guidelines developed in the planning phase and in response to the needs and interests of the intended audience.

7. Pupils use technology as appropriate in order to enhance their presentations and reports.

8. Pupils share their final report/project with larger groups, with other classes, in the community and/or with family.

9. The teacher identifies and shares the evaluation criteria for the process and the product.

10. Pupils are involved in setting evaluation criteria for the process and the product.

11. Pupils provide appropriate self-evaluation and peer evaluation of the final product and the inquiry process.

12. Pupils monitor and adapt their own inquiry skills and strategies during the process.

13. Pupils share their feelings and progress each lesson.

14. Teacher monitors progress at the end of each lesson.

15. Pupils talk about what went well and what was challenging.

Part Four

Homework

CHAPTER EIGHT

Homework

What's the point of homework?

Homework has had a rough ride in recent years with many teachers and parents calling for it to be scrapped completely. Those who fail to see the merits of homework tend to cite John Hattie's book 'Visible Learning' which gives homework an effect size of 0.26, meaning there's only a 21% chance that homework will make a positive difference to a pupil's levels of progress.

One prominent advocate of scrapping homework is Tim Lott of The Guardian who, in October 2012, admitted to "a profound dislike of homework" and asked "Why do we torment kids in this way?" He went on to say:

> "I had no homework during my primary school years and very little during the first years of grammar school. This was the norm in the 1960s and 70s. At some point since, the work "ethic" that has infected national life generally – not that it's particularly ethical – insists that if you're not working, you're doing something faintly dissolute or purposeless, even if you're six.

> "Nothing is more precious than those islands of childhood that are left untouched by invading adults and their fund of schemes

for the future when you finally make it as a "worthy citizen". Let children drift and dream and make up games with plastic guns and My Little Pony, watch unsuitable TV and stare out the window. But this makes evangelists for the work society uneasy."

Lott, in turn, cites Sara Bennet and Nancy Kalish who - in their book 'The Case Against Homework' point out that "all the credible research on homework suggests that for younger kids, homework has no connection with positive learning outcomes and for older kids, the benefits of homework level off sharply after the first couple of assignments."

Homework generates conflict with parents, Lott says, and, worse still, parents are required to help. The problem is, most parents are not trained teachers and are often impatient and ineffective.

The end result of homework, according to Lott and many others, is that study becomes associated in the young mind with conflict and unhappiness.

But the facts are a little more nuanced. It's probably true that too much homework - particularly if it's meaningless 'fluff' - for Lott's 10-year-old daughter is pointless, counterproductive and switches her and her parents off education. But that's not the whole story. The benefits of homework vary by age; the older the pupil, the greater the benefit. Indeed, if you look in detail at what Hattie says in 'Visible Learning', you'll see that behind the headline figure of 0.26 are two separate figures, one for primary and one for secondary and those two figures are startlingly different.

But first let's take a look at effect sizes in general. An effect size of 0.2 is considered small. An effect size of 0.4 is considered medium. An effect size of 0.6 is considered large. Anything greater than 0.4 is therefore above average and anything above 0.6 is classed as excellent.

Hattie says that the effect of homework on pupil outcomes is 0.26 overall but is 0.15 at primary and 0.64 at secondary. Therefore, it is small at primary but large at secondary. In other words, the effect of homework on pupil outcomes in the primary phase is, as Lott and others rightly argue, negligible and could do more harm than good if it's not managed well. But the effect of homework on pupil outcomes in the secondary phase of education is excellent and therefore well worth persevering with, albeit improving. Homework, then, is not to be disregarded quite so quickly.

Hattie also goes into some detail about the kinds of homework that work best. The highest effects, he says, are associated with practice and rehearsal tasks. And short, frequent homework tasks which are closely monitored by the teacher have the most impact on pupil progress.

The optimal time per night for pupils to spend on homework also varies by age; the older the pupil, the more time they should spend on homework. This is an imperfect science but, roughly, I would argue that the following is a good guide: pupils in the primary phase should do no more than about 20 minutes homework a night, pupils in Key Stage 3 should do about 40 minutes, pupils in Key Stage 4 should do about 60 minutes, and pupils in Key Stage 5 (post-16) should do about 90 minutes a night.

What homework works best?

In my experience, homework - like all forms of assignment - works best when you give pupils a clear picture of the final product and a real audience for their work. Homework also works best when you allow a certain degree of autonomy, whereby pupils can make choices about which tasks they carry out, how they carry them out and how they will be assessed on the final product. And homework also works best when you incorporate cultural products into it such as TV, film, magazines, food, and sports - to name but five examples - in order to engage pupils' personal interests and awaken prior knowledge.

Naturally, it is always best to avoid 'fluff' assignments - homework tasks which bear no relation to what is being learnt and which simply waste pupils' time. My daughter recently baked a cake in the shape of a wind turbine for a science project. It took her five hours. Needless to say, I was less than impressed. What aspect of science did she practice, rehearse or consolidate during those five hours, I asked her. She struggled for an answer. 'But I like baking,' came her eventual reply. Homework must have genuine purpose and the 'doing' must be linked to the 'learning' because pupils remember what they are asked to do more than what they are asked to think about.

It is also wise to try vary the language of homework tasks, perhaps by using Bloom's taxonomy. Rather than always asking pupils simple comprehension questions or to summarise a text, try to move up and down the taxonomy by asking them to: define, recall, describe, label, identify, match, name, or state (knowledge); translate, predict, explain, summarise, describe, compare, or classify (comprehension); demonstrate how, solve, use, interpret, relate, or apply (application); analyse, explain, infer, break down, prioritise, reason logically, or draw conclusions (analysis); design, create, compose, combine, reorganise, reflect, predict, speculate, hypothesise, or summarise (synthesis); assess, judge, compare/contrast, or evaluate (evaluation).

Homework, if it is to be taken seriously, should be non-negotiable like class-work. As such, you should not allow 'passes' whereby pupils can be excused from handing homework in and you should require everyone to 'turn in a paper' so even when someone has forgotten to bring their homework in to school on the due-date they should be required to write their name on a piece of paper and the reason they haven't got their homework and submit that instead. Then, crucially, at the bottom of the page they should add their parent's name and daytime phone number. That way you have a paper from everyone, a record of who hasn't handed their homework in on time and a way of contacting parents to make them aware of their child's failure to comply with the rules. I'm sure you'll find the tactic of requiring pupils to submit their parents' phone numbers will quickly have the desired effect.

Occasionally, homework could be integrated with other subjects, becoming cross-curricular and thematic, enabling pupils to see the natural links that exist between subjects and the transferability of key skills, as well as to provide variety. This could occur once every half term as an extended project.

Types of homework

Broadly speaking there are four types of homework task:

1. Practice
2. Preparation
3. Study
4. Extend or elaborate

Of these, practice is the most valuable in terms of producing measurable academic gains because practice builds proficiency and mastery. Practice can be single skill or cumulative. Cumulative practice is where a new skill is practised alongside a previously-learnt skill. A pupil must have demonstrated competence in the skill being practised before being asked to do it for homework. Homework should not - except in the case of flipped learning, which we will discuss in a moment - introduce new concepts or information.

There are three forms of practice worth considering for homework tasks:

1. Spaced repetition. This is where information is learnt initially then repeated again several times at increasingly long intervals so that pupils get to the point of almost forgetting what they've learnt and have to delve into their long-term memories to retrieve their prior knowledge, thus strengthening those memories. This is because a memory is a neural connection and thoughts and experiences build connections between the billions of neurones in our brains, establishing new networks and patterns. Neural connections fade away if they are neglected but can get stronger with repeated use because repetition leads to neural habits of thought. In other words, the more often we repeat learning, the better the information will be learnt. But that's not all. As well as returning to prior learning following an interval, we should explore that information in a new way because making new associations further strengthens our memories, hence homework task number two...

2. Retrieval practice. This is testing or quizzing (such as multiple choice) used not for the purposes of assessment but for reinforcement and to provide pupils with feedback information on what they know and don't yet know so that they can better focus their future studies. As I explained above, a memory is a neural connection which fades away if it is neglected but can get stronger with repeated use. The more often we repeat learning, the better the information is learnt. As well as returning to prior learning following an interval, we should explore that information in a new way because making new associations further strengthens our memories.

The number of different connections we make influences the number of times memories are revisited, which in turn influences the length of time we retain a memory. When we connect different pieces of information with each other, we retain them for longer, because we retrieve them more often. It follows, then, that the more often we connect what we are teaching today to what we taught previously, the better the information will be learnt. If we retrieve a memory in order to connect prior knowledge to new information, the memory is strengthened even further so using quizzes in which the information is presented in new ways helps pupils to improve their learning. We could also plan opportunities for our pupils to reorganise the information they've learnt by writing about it or talking about it.

3. *Cognitive disfluency* (otherwise known as desirable difficulties). This is a memory technique that makes learning stick by placing artificial barriers in the way of pupils' learning. Doing this means that the process of encoding (initial learning) is made harder so that the process of retrieval (recalling that learning later, say in a test) is made easier. One example of a desirable difficulty is making learning materials less easy to read, perhaps by using a difficult to decipher font, in order to make pupils think harder about the content. Another example is to use more complex language when forming questions and tasks so that pupils have to think harder about what is being asked of them before tackling the work.

*

Before we move on to *flipped learning*, let's conclude with some general homework do's and don'ts:

Don't:

- Use a one size fits all approach - homework should be differentiated to meet individual pupil needs
- Set homework that contains new information - it should be used to practice taught skills
- Set homework too quickly at the end of a lesson - time needs to be spent explaining it
- Collect homework in but not review it - it needs to be assessed and feedback given
- Give out homework that has no purpose or objective

Do:

- Give less homework but more often
- Have a specific purpose for every homework task you set; don't set 'busy work'
- Ensure that homework is engaging
- Allot sufficient time in the lesson to present and explain the homework
- Answer pupils' questions about the homework and check their understanding
- Articulate the rationale for the homework and how it will be assessed
- Provide timely feedback on what has been mastered and what still needs to be practised
- Provide choices about the homework task, format and presentation

*

Flipped learning

One increasingly popular form of homework - and indeed learning in general - is flipped learning.

Flipped learning, as the name suggests, 'flips' on its head the traditional idea of the classroom being used for lectures and the home being used for answering questions about that lecture.

Flipped learning effectively redefines homework because assignments involve video lectures which are viewed at home (or during private study time in school for pupils who don't have Internet access at home) as many times as pupils wish in order to digest difficult concepts. Class time is then freed up for pupils to ask questions and participate in collaborative work.

Flipped learning changes the distribution of teacher time. In a traditional classroom the teacher tends to engage more with those pupils who ask questions rather than those who do not. But it is those who do not who invariably need the most help. Flipped learning ensures that the teacher's time is more fairly distributed.

When flipped learning is used, it is important that learning materials are varied rather than relying solely on video lectures which can quickly become repetitive and switch pupils off. Instead, teachers can use audio files and reading materials as well as video, and can source these from a variety of organisations including the Khan Academy and TED.

It is important, as with any task that relies on the use of technology, that there is fair access in school and that sufficient time is allowed between a homework being set and then being collected for pupils to access the materials.

Finally, the shorter the videos, audio files or reading materials, (3-6 minutes is ideal), the more likely it is that pupils will engage with the material and watch, listen or read them more than once, thus strengthening their learning. If the material is short, more flipped learning tasks can be set, too, in order to move the classroom learning forwards at a more rapid pace.

In Chapter Nine we will examine ways of making Key Stage 3 assessment and feedback more effective in order to expedite the progress made by pupils and close the gap between different groups of pupils. But first, in another **bonus chapter** exclusive to this edition of the book, we examine the habits of academic success...

BONUS CHAPTER

What are the habits of academic success?

I don't believe in conspiracy theories but Abraham Lincoln and John F Kennedy have always made my spine tingle. After all, they have an awful lot in common...

Abraham Lincoln was elected to Congress in 1846; John F. Kennedy was elected to Congress in 1946. Abraham Lincoln was elected president in 1860; John F Kennedy was elected president in 1960. The names Lincoln and Kennedy each contain seven letters. Both men were particularly concerned with civil rights. Both their wives lost children while living in the White House. Both presidents were shot on a Friday. Both were shot in the head. Lincoln's secretary, Kennedy, warned him not to go to the theatre; Kennedy's secretary, Lincoln, warned him not to go to Dallas. Both were assassinated by Southerners. Both were succeeded by Southerners. Both successors were named Johnson: Andrew Johnson, who succeeded Lincoln, was born in 1808; Lyndon Johnson, who succeeded Kennedy, was born in 1908. Both assassins were known by three names which comprised 15 letters: John Wilkes Booth was born in 1839; Lee Harvey Oswald was born in 1939. Having assassinated

Lincoln, Booth ran from the theatre and was caught in a warehouse; having assassinated Kennedy, Oswald ran from a warehouse and was caught in a theatre. Both Booth and Oswald were assassinated before their trials.

Spooky, eh? I don't know about you, but the hairs on the back of my neck are standing up. But, as I say, I don't believe in conspiracy theories. I do, however, believe in coincidence. So what's the difference? When you think about it, coincidences aren't spooky at all; they are, in fact, perfectly rational because they express a simple, logical pattern of cause and effect. Take, for example, academic achievement...

Several years ago, while working as a deputy headteacher, I interviewed fifty pupils in years 11 and 13 who had achieved high grades in their GCSE and A level exams. I found something spooky – a series of apparent coincidences. For example...

All the pupils I interviewed had an attendance of more than 93 per cent; 90 per cent of them had a perfect attendance record. All the pupils I interviewed told me they used their planners regularly and considered themselves to be well-organised. As a result, all the pupils I interviewed completed their homework on time and without fail. All the pupils I interviewed told me they always asked for help from their teachers when they got stuck. They didn't regard doing so as a sign of weakness, rather a sign of strength. Admitting they didn't know something and asking questions meant they learnt something new and increased their intelligence.

Most of the pupils I interviewed were involved in clubs, sports, or hobbies at lunchtime, after school and/or at weekends. Though not all were sporting, they did all have get-up-and-go attitudes. They didn't spend every evening and weekend watching television. They were sociable and, in order to unwind, they read books. Lots of books. In fact, the school library confirmed that my cohort of high-achievers were among the biggest borrowers in school. All the pupils believed that doing well in school would increase their chances of getting higher paid and more interesting jobs later in life.

Many of them had a clear idea about the kind of job they wanted to do and knew what was needed in order to get it. They had researched the entry requirements and had then mapped out the necessary school, college, and/or university paths. They had connected what they were doing in school with achieving their future ambitions. School work and good exam results had a purpose, they were means to an important end.

Was it spooky that nearly all these high-achieving pupils had done the same things? Or was it a simple case of cause and effect: because these pupils shared these traits they went on to succeed? I believe it was the latter: it was because these pupils had attended school, were well organised, completed work on time, and had an end goal in mind that they had achieved excellent grades in their final exams. The cause was diligent study and determination; the effect was high achievement. As such, these young people can teach our pupils a valuable lesson - that the recipe for success is to:

- Have good attendance and punctuality.
- Be organised and complete all work on time.
- Be willing to ask for help when you're stuck.
- Have something to aim for and be ambitious.
- Map out your career path and be determined to succeed.

I now wish to explore the second of these ingredients in more detail: personal organisation. One means of becoming better organised is to acquire effective study skills. According to Paul C Brown et al in *Make It Stick*, the following study skills are proven to be particularly helpful to pupils...

1. Self-quizzing

Self-quizzing is about retrieving knowledge and skills from memory and is far more effective than simply re-reading a text. When your pupils read a text or study notes, you should teach them to pause periodically to ask themselves questions – without looking in the text – such as:

- What are the key ideas?
- What terms or ideas are new to me? How would I define them?
- How do the ideas in this text relate to what I already know?

You should set aside a little time every week for your pupils to quiz themselves on the current week's work and the material you have covered in previous weeks. Once they have self-quizzed, get your pupils to check their answers and make sure they have an accurate understanding of what they know and what they don't know. Your pupils need to know that making mistakes will not set them back, so long as they check their answers later and correct any errors.

You should space out your pupils' retrieval practice. This means studying information more than once and leaving increasingly large gaps between practice sessions. Initially, new material should be revisited within a day or so then not again for several days or a week. When your pupils are feeling surer of certain material, they should quiz themselves on it once a month. They should also interleave the study of two or more topics so that alternating between them requires them to continually refresh their memories of each topic.

2. Elaboration

Elaboration is the process of finding additional layers of meaning in new material. It involves relating new material to what pupils already know, explaining it to somebody else, or explaining how it relates to the wider world. An effective form of elaboration is to use a metaphor or image for the new material.

3. Generation

Generation is when pupils attempt to answer a question or solve a problem before being shown the answer or the solution. The act of filling in a missing word (the cloze test) results in better learning and a stronger memory of the text than simply reading the text. Before reading new class material, ask pupils to explain the key ideas they expect to find and how they expect these ideas will relate to their prior knowledge.

4. Reflection

Reflection involves taking a moment to review what has been learned. Pupils ask questions such as:
- What went well? What could have gone better?
- What other knowledge or experience does it remind me of?
- What might I need to learn in order to achieve better mastery?
- What strategies could I use next time to get better results?

5. Calibration

Calibration is achieved when pupils adjust their judgment to reflect reality – in other words, they become certain that their sense of what they know and can do is accurate. Often when we revise information, we look at a question and convince ourselves that we know the answer, then move on to the next question without making an effort to actually answer the previous one. If we do not write down an answer, we may create the illusion of knowing when in fact we would have difficulty giving a response. We need to teach our pupils to remove the illusion of knowing and actually answer all the questions even if they think they know the answer and that it is too easy.

Here are some other useful study skills we could teach our pupils:

1. Anticipate test questions during lessons.
2. Read study guides, find terms they can't recall or don't know and learn them.
3. Copy key terms and their definitions into a notebook.
4. Take practice tests.
5. Reorganise class material into a study guide.
6. Copy out key concepts and regularly test themselves on them.
7. Space out revision and practice activities.

And here are some handy tips to help our pupils to study smarter:

Create desirable difficulties in the classroom by using tests frequently. Design study tools that make use of retrieval practice, generation and elaboration.

Return to concepts covered earlier in the term. Space, interleave and vary the topics covered in class so that pupils frequently have to "reload" what they already know about each topic in order to determine how new material relates to, or indeed differs from, prior knowledge.

Make learning transparent by helping your pupils to understand the ways in which you have incorporated desirable difficulties and other strategies into your lessons.

Plan for "free recall", whereby pupils spend 10 minutes at the end of each lesson filling a blank piece of paper with everything they can remember from that lesson.

Set a weekly homework whereby pupils create summary sheets (perhaps a side of A4) on which they summarise the previous week's learning in text, annotated illustrations, or graphical organisers. The purpose of this task is to stimulate retrieval and reflection, and to capture the previous week's learning before it is lost.

And finally, **explain how learning works**. Help your pupils to understand that creating some kinds of difficulties during the learning process helps to strengthen learning and memory because when learning is easy it is often superficial and soon forgotten. Help your pupils to understand that not all intellectual abilities are innate – in fact, when learning is "effortful", it changes the brain, making new connections and increasing intellectual ability. Pupils learn better when they struggle with new problems by themselves before being shown the solution, not vice-versa. Help your pupils to understand that, in order to achieve excellence, they must strive to surpass their current level of ability. This, by its very nature, often leads to set-backs and set-backs are often what provide the information that's needed in order to achieve mastery.

Part Five

Assessment

CHAPTER NINE

Assessment

One in four children in the UK grows up in poverty. The attainment gap between rich and poor is detectable at an early age (22 months) and widens throughout the education system. Children from the lowest income homes are half as likely to get five good GCSEs and go on to higher education. White working class pupils (particularly boys) are amongst the lowest performers. The link between poverty and attainment is multi-racial with socio-economic gaps much greater than those between different ethnic groups.

Effective assessment, tracking and feedback is essential throughout Key Stage 3 in order to ensure that every pupil achieves his or her potential and that attainment gaps are not allowed to widen. And yet, in a majority of its inspections between 2013 and 2015, Ofsted found many schools neglect these three years of a child's education and are then forced to take remedial action at Key Stage 4.

As we already know, Ofsted's 2015 report KS3: The Wasted Years? claims that Key Stage 3 is not a high priority for secondary school leaders in terms of timetabling, assessment and the monitoring of pupils' progress. It also says that school leaders prioritise the pastoral over the academic needs of pupils during pupils' transition from primary school and that many secondary schools do not build sufficiently on pupils' prior learning. Finally, the report argues that schools are not using Pupil Premium funding effectively to close gaps quickly in Key Stage 3.

So how can schools improve the quality and effectiveness of assessment at Key Stage 3? How can they ensure that every pupil's progress is monitored and that interventions are put into place in a timely manner as soon as a pupil's progress falters? And how can schools be sure that those interventions are the most effective strategies to use and offer the best value for money for the public purse?

Using data

In an earlier chapter in this book on cross-phase partnerships I explained that data is more than just a spreadsheet, it is a conversation. Whereas most secondary teachers will already have access to some information about their new Year 7s including which primary school they came from, the scaled scores they achieved on their Key Stage 2 tests and, if they delve into the question level analysis, the marks they received for individual questions in those tests, a pupil's Year 6 teacher will know so much more than these numbers can possibly say. They'll know, for example, what the pupil is capable of achieving when they're not under test conditions and what particular topics they've studied and found interesting. They'll know what their attitude to learning is like and what skills they've developed over their first seven years of schooling. They'll know what extra-curricular activities they've taken part in and how well they did, as well as what motivates them to succeed and what demotivates them. They'll know, too, what their home life is like and what obstacles they've had to overcome and might still be facing on a daily basis. So, yes, data is more than a spreadsheet. Recognising assessment in its widest sense - and taking information from as many sources as possible - enables data to become a rich and meaningful conversation.

The effective use of data - to monitor and evaluate pupil progress and facilitate these rich conversations - lies at the heart of good assessment. But what does it look like in practice?

Good data management means identifying and unpicking the data in order to analyse the progress of pupil groups. Good data management means auditing the effectiveness of past and current interventions. Good data management means discussing barriers with staff and pupils, asking them what do they think are the priorities. It means raising the profile of research and potential solutions, using external evidence of what works, identifying the tools and strategies that are needed.

Good data management means building leadership capacity to make sustainable improvements and strengthen the school's own performance capability. It means developing a plan and demonstrating the links to the school's core aims.

Data in Key Stage 3 needs to be used to close the gaps between the performances of different groups of pupils, particularly - as we heard at the start of this chapter - those from disadvantaged socio-economic backgrounds. So how can we do this?

Closing the gap

Firstly, when it comes to closing the gap between the educational achievement of different groups of pupils, what matters most is pedagogy - if we get the teaching and learning in the classroom right first time, then there is less need of interventions later. In particular, what works best at Key Stage 3 for closing the gap is structured phonics instruction, cooperative learning approaches, frequent assessment and feedback, and the explicit teaching of metacognition. Contrary to popular opinion, the traditional use of ICT in the classroom has only modest gains although the use of whole-class ICT (such as the interactive whiteboard, embedded multimedia, etc) is more effective than the use of individualised, self-instructional ICT programmes. Classroom management strategies - such as the use of a rapid pace of instruction, all-pupil responses, and a common language of discipline - help to close the gap, too, as does the use of one to one tutoring for struggling readers.

Other proven whole-school approaches to closing the gap include:
- Rigorous monitoring and the use of data
- Raising pupil aspirations using engagement programmes
- Engaging parents and raising parental aspirations
- Developing social and emotional competencies
- Coaching teachers and teaching assistants in specific strategies such as cooperative learning, frequent assessment and metacognition

In order to close the gap, school leaders need to ensure that there is enhanced collaboration and communication between staff both within and between partner schools. This may necessitate the development of leadership skills among some staff and helping teachers to improve their understanding of alternative contexts and ways of dealing with similar issues. Teachers may also need help developing a better awareness of the barriers to learning that some pupils face and an understanding of the attainment gaps. Another important strategy for closing the gap is to increase parental involvement, both in terms of enlisting their support with homework and in helping to raise pupil aspirations and expectations.

Life after levels

Assessment in Key Stage 3 should emulate that in Key Stage 4 - in other words, there should be the same rigour and determination to assess, monitor and track pupil progress in Years 7, 8 and 9 as there is in Years 10 and 11, and the tracking data should be used just as frequently and robustly to identify pupils whose progress has faltered and to put in place intervention strategies to support them.

However, there is one key difference. At Key Stage 4 assessment takes the form of GCSE grades. At Key Stage 3, life has been made a little more complicated by the scrapping of national curriculum levels as a statutory requirement. So let us take a look at what the government says about assessment in Key Stage 3 now that we live in a life after levels...

The Department for Education has made clear that each school is autonomous and can develop its own system of assessment. Whatever system it develops should be fair and transparent, and it should set high expectations for the attainment and progress of all pupils. The Department for Education says that assessment should be the servant and not the master of excellent teaching and, what matters most, is that schools provide high value qualifications and teach a broad and balanced curriculum.

In Years 7 and 8, schools are expected to engage in ongoing formative assessment of pupils although this is not a statutory requirement. They are also expected to provide periodic progress checks (again, this is non-statutory). Schools are also expected to summatively assess pupils against end of year outcomes although, once again, this is non-statutory. In fact, the only statutory duty in Years 7 and 8 is to report once a year to parents in some form.

In Year 9, schools are also expected to engage in ongoing

formative assessment which is again a not a statutory duty. They are also expected to provide periodic progress checks (again, this is non-statutory). The key difference is that, in Year 9, the expectation that schools summatively assess pupils against end of key stage outcomes is a statutory requirement, as is the requirement to report to parents.

Although the statutory duties placed on schools are somewhat limited, it is good practice to ensure that pupil progress is regularly observed and analysed and that the data is shared with all interested parties - parents, staff and governors. It is also good practice to ensure that the data that is gathered from this process is used - not just to report progress - but in a number of other important ways. For example, progress data should be used to identify underperforming groups and then to direct the appropriate deployment of staff and resources to support those groups to close the gap. Progress data should also be used to inform teachers' target-setting activity, ensuring targets are aspirational but achievable. Finally, progress data should be used to monitor the impact of strategies and interventions and those interventions which are found not to be working well enough should be stopped or improved and then re-evaluated.

In the best schools, there are well-developed pupil tracking systems at work in Key Stage 3 as well as in Key Stage 4 which capture a wider range of data than just attainment levels. These schools also use external data and self-evaluation in order to focus on the gaps and on pupil progress, not just on average attainment. As well as informing staff on pupil progress, these schools use data to provide pupils with regular feedback on their progress.

Let's take a closer look at how your school might respond to 'life after levels'...

Why replace levels?

The Commission for Assessment Without Levels, in their 2015 report, claimed that the use of levels led to a curriculum driven by targets which, in turn, came to dominate all forms of in-school assessment and had a profoundly negative impact on teaching and learning.

As a result, progress - they said - became synonymous with moving up to the next 'level' or 'sub-level'. But this posed a problem: progress - in real terms - involves developing a deeper and broader understanding of subject matter, not simply moving on to work that affords a greater level of difficulty.

The Commission also said that, as a consequence of National Curriculum levels becoming synonymous with assessment, the more informal, everyday formative assessment that should always have been an integral part of effective teaching at Key Stage 3 was largely abandoned. Instead, teachers were simply tracking pupils' progress towards target levels rather than engaging in genuine dialogue with pupils about what they had mastered and what they still needed to practice.

One of the other problems with this approach was that the language of levels did not lend itself to assessing the underpinning knowledge and understanding of a concept. Level descriptors offered pseudo-scientific and ostensibly precise measurements which, when analysed, offer little help to pupils in their quest to know how to improve.

Removing the 'label' of levels, the Commission suggested, could help to improve pupils' mindsets about their own ability...

Once levels have been removed, teachers - in reviewing their teaching and assessment strategies - could then aim to ensure that they used methods that allowed all pupils full access to the curriculum.

The Commission also claimed that the expectation

placed on teachers to collect data in order to track pupils' progress towards target levels and sub-levels considerably increases teachers' workloads. Without levels, the Commission said, teachers would gradually increase their confidence in using a wider range of formative assessment strategies without the burden of unnecessary recording and tracking.

Removing levels would also shine a brighter spotlight on high quality formative assessment, thereby improving the quality of teaching, as well as contributing to raising standards and reinforcing schools' freedoms to deliver a quality education in the way that best suits the needs of their pupils and the strengths and skills of their staff.

The Commission therefore recommended that schools developed an alternative to levels that marked a definitive departure from the prevailing culture rather than replicated the existing system in all but name. They strongly hinted that schools should base their new assessment systems on the mastery learning approach developed by Benjamin Bloom in the 1960s. This makes sense because the new National Curriculum also has mastery learning at its core.

In Bloom's version of 'mastery', learning is broken down into discrete units and is presented in a logical order. Pupils are required to demonstrate a comprehensive knowledge of each unit before being allowed to move on to the next unit, the assumption being that all pupils will achieve this level of mastery if they are appropriately supported: some may take longer and need more help, but all will get there in the end.

Designing a new system

In a moment we will explore how a school could build a new assessment system to replace levels based on the concept of mastery learning but first we must take a step back...

Before a school can agree a new assessment system - whether it designs one in-house or purchases one 'off the peg' so to speak - it should make sure it has written, consulted upon and agreed a whole-school assessment policy. This policy should then be ratified by the governing body or academy sponsors. From this point forwards, the assessment policy should be the school's guiding light; everything the school does to develop an alternative to levels should support the delivery of this policy.

Once a new assessment policy is in place, a school needs to decide what unit of measurement will replace National Curriculum levels. In other words, how will the school describe pupils' learning and progress? Whatever measure a school decides to use, it must successfully quantify learning and progress and must do so in a more meaningful way than levels and sub-levels did, or else why change?

So where should a school start?

Some schools I've worked with or spoken to during the course of writing this book have made the mistake of developing a new assessment system - and grade descriptors to quantify pupil performance - on the false assumption that their existing schemes of work will adequately cover the Subject Content in the new National Curriculum. In other words, they have begun by designing a new unit of measurement to replace levels *before* considering how they will plan and teach the new National Curriculum. The result has been a system of 'levels' in all but name.

Schools should start by engaging in a process of detailed curriculum planning *before* they set about designing a system of assessment. After all, how can you decide on your assessment criteria before you know what it is you're assessing? How we teach the National Curriculum and how pupils respond to it should form the basis of any new assessment system and that system should be based on new schemes of work. Those schemes of work should, in turn, be written in line with the new National Curriculum.

What's more, assessment systems which simply recreate grading similar to levels and sub-levels are, to my mind, missing the point.

*

The new National Curriculum is a description of the content that must be taught in each subject and should, therefore, be a school's starting point in deciding upon the units of measurement it will use to quantify learning and progress.

A school's first task, therefore, should be to convert the content described in the National Curriculum into schemes of work which describe what will be taught and what learning will result. This kind of detailed curriculum planning is necessary if a school is to successfully develop assessment criteria. Schools should not make the mistake of rushing into designing a new assessment system before they've considered how the National Curriculum will be taught in practice.

A school's second task, then, is to understand how a pupil's knowledge and skills in those parts of the subject covered in a particular scheme of work will accumulate over the course of Key Stage 3 into an holistic understanding of the concepts, key ideas, and capabilities learnt in the subject. As such, schemes of work need to be progressive in nature, developing gradually over time.

Only once the National Curriculum has been converted into schemes of work and everyone is clear about how pupils' knowledge and skills will develop over the course of those schemes of work, can a school move on to the third and final task: to develop a means of describing and quantifying what pupils are learning as they move through the schemes of work.

So, to summarise:

1. Convert the National Curriculum into schemes of work covering the year and key stage
2. Understand how knowledge and skills will accumulate over the year and key stage
3. Develop a system for describing and quantifying pupils' learning in each scheme of work, year and key stage

Let's now turn our attentions to how this will work in practice and to how we might quantify pupils' learning...

Putting it into practice

The Commission for Assessment Without Levels were clear in their report that 'life after levels' should be less bureaucratic for teachers. Teachers should spent more time engaged in formative classroom assessments with pupils and less time tracking and recording data. As such, a majority of the assessments that take place in Key Stage 3 should be informal, leading to diagnostic feedback given to pupils either in writing in their exercise books or verbally in lessons. Naturally, this data will either be unrecorded or held locally in teachers' mark-books.

Diagnostic feedback should be comment-only and be specific about what pupils need to do in order to improve. In an earlier chapter about the Conditions for Learning, I explained that the best feedback addresses faulty interpretations and comments on rather than grades work. I also said that the best feedback provides cues or prompts for further work, is timely, specific and clear, and is focused on task and process rather than on praising. Feedback also works best when it is explicit about the marking criteria, offers suggestions for improvement, and is focused on how pupils can close the gap between their current and their desired performance; it does not focus on presentation or quantity of work.

Occasionally, however, it will be necessary for teachers to reflect on how well their pupils are responding to what is being taught and to share this information more formally with their subject leaders, senior leaders, and other colleagues who teach the same class. This more formal assessment will need to take the form of progress against or towards targets - or perhaps age-related expectations - so what should it look like in practice?

The use of levels and sub-levels assumed that pupils scaled the mountain of progress in a uniform manner in response to teaching, and that we could measure each step with accuracy then categorise and label each pupil accordingly.

Mastery learning replaces this rush to hike up the mountainside with the belief that all pupils will comprehensively know and understand the learning from each unit before moving on to the next. Progress, therefore, tends to be non-linear and tailored to meet the needs of each pupil.

'Progress' is a complex concept - a dotted line used to summarise the overall path taken along the mountainside, snaking towards the peak, which may go up as well as down as pupils find the right terrain and get a solid foothold in the rock. But, statistically-speaking, we can estimate the average grade that a pupil is capable of achieving based on their prior performance and this information can be used to notify us if pupils fall below expectations.

Intended learning outcomes provide a good starting start - a foundation, if you like - for tracking pupil progress because they summarise what is taught in each lesson or unit and they are already widely used in lesson planning and delivery. Teachers routinely write and share objectives with pupils at the start of lessons and use them to measure progress in lesson plenaries.

As long as intended learning outcomes cover all the statements in the National Curriculum Subject Content, then tracking and recording pupils' acquisition of them should provide a cumulative assessment log which will quantify their progress at any given point during Key Stage 3.

Once we reach the end of a scheme of work, or a sensible waypoint in a unit, a good way to express the extent to which pupils have mastered a set of intended learning outcomes is to categorise them as either 'Emerging', 'Developing', 'Secure' or 'Mastered'. Using only four categories like this - as opposed to myriad levels and sub-levels - provides a broad brush approach which contrasts with the artificial precision provided by level descriptors.

These four categories can then by linked to GCSE grades to show the degree to which a pupil is 'GCSE ready'. For example, the word 'Emerging' could equate to GCSE grades 1 and 2, whilst 'Developing' could be pegged to GCSE grades 3 and 4. 'Secure', meanwhile, could be equivalent to GCSE grades 5 and 6, whereas 'Mastered' could equate to GCSE grades 7, 8 and 9.

In Chapter Ten we will continue to explore assessment at Key Stage 3 and focus on the use of the Pupil Premium.

CHAPTER TEN

The Pupil Premium

What is the Pupil Premium and how can it be spent?

The Pupil Premium is money given to schools to help disadvantaged pupils. Ofsted said that schools prioritise their Pupil Premium spending in Key Stage 4 and do not use the funding effectively in Key Stage 3 to ensure that gaps between disadvantaged pupils and their peers continue to close following the transition to secondary school. However, this is a vicious cycle because if you focus your time and resources in Key Stage 4, and thus neglect Key Stage 3, then the gap will widen in the intervening years and that time and money will be needed simply to compensate for ineffective practice in the earlier phase of secondary education. If, however, the Pupil Premium is used effectively at Key Stage 3 and pupils are supported through high quality teaching and interventions, then they will be provided with a better springboard to GCSE and fewer remedial actions will be needed in Years 10 and 11.

Before we look at how the Pupil Premium might best be utilised in Key Stage 3, let's be clear on who the funding is for and how it can legally be spent...

Pupil Premium funding is awarded to pupils who are categorised as 'Ever 6 FSM'. For the 2015/16 academic year, for example, the funding will be given to pupils who are recorded in the January 2015 school census who are known to have been eligible for free school meals (FSM) in any of the previous six years (in other words, since the summer of 2009), as well as those first known to be eligible in January 2015.

Pupil Premium funding is also awarded to pupils who are adopted from care or who have left care. For the 2015/16 academic year, for example, the funding will be given to pupils who are recorded in the January 2015 school census and alternative provision census who were looked after by an English or Welsh local authority immediately before being adopted, or who left local authority care on a special guardianship order or child arrangements order (previously known as a residence order).

Finally, Pupil Premium funding is awarded to pupils who are categorised as 'Ever 5 service child' which - for the purposes of the Pupil Premium grant conditions - means a pupil recorded in the January 2015 school census who was eligible for the service child premium in any of the previous four years (in other words, since the January 2011 school census) as well as those recorded as a service child for the first time on the January 2015 school census.

Pupil Premium is for the purposes of the school it is awarded to. In other words, it is for the educational benefit of pupils registered at that school. But it can also be used for the benefit of pupils registered at other maintained schools or academies and on community facilities such as services whose provision furthers any charitable purpose for the benefit of pupils at the school or their families, or people who live or work in the locality in which the school is situated. The money does not have to be completely spent by schools in the financial year it is awarded; some or all of it may be carried forward to future financial years.

The Pupil Premium and Ofsted

Schools are held to account for how they spend the money and the impact that money has on closing the gap. For example, Ofsted inspections report on how a school's use of the funding affects the attainment of their disadvantaged pupils and the DfE holds a school to account through performance tables, which include data on the attainment of pupils who attract the funding, the progress made by these pupils, and the gap in attainment between disadvantaged pupils and their peers.

Ofsted's Common Inspection Handbook (2015) explains that when judging the effectiveness of leadership and management, inspectors will consider: "How effectively leaders use additional funding, including the pupil premium, and measure its impact on outcomes for pupils, and how effectively governors hold them to account for this."

The Pupil Premium is also mentioned in the grade descriptors for leadership and management. The 'outstanding' grade descriptors, for example, include the following: *"Governors systematically challenge senior leaders so that the effective deployment of staff and resources, including the pupil premium and special educational needs (SEN) funding, secures excellent outcomes for pupils. Governors do not shy away from challenging leaders about variations in outcomes for pupil groups, especially between disadvantaged and other pupils."* In the 'good' grade descriptors, meanwhile, it says: *"Governors hold senior leaders stringently to account for all aspects of the school's performance, including the use of pupil premium and*

SEN funding, ensuring that the skilful deployment of staff and resources delivers good or improving outcomes for pupils."

When preparing for an inspection, the lead inspector will analyse information on the school's website, including its statement on the use of the Pupil Premium. The lead inspector will also request that any reports following an external review of the school's use of the Pupil Premium are made available at the start of the inspection. During the inspection, inspectors will gather evidence about the use of the Pupil Premium in relation to the following: The level of Pupil Premium funding received by the school that academic year and in previous years; how the school has spent the money and why it has decided to spend it in the way it has; and any differences made to the learning and progress of disadvantaged pupils as shown by outcomes data and inspection evidence.

Inspectors will take particular account of the progress made by disadvantaged pupils by the end of the key stage compared with that made nationally by other pupils with similar starting points and the extent to which any gaps in this progress, and consequently in attainment, are closing. Inspectors will compare the progress and attainment of the school's disadvantaged pupils with the national figures for the progress and attainment of non-disadvantaged pupils. They will then consider in-school gaps between disadvantaged and non-disadvantaged pupils, and how much these gaps are closing. Inspectors will consider in-school gaps between disadvantaged and non-disadvantaged pupils.

It's worth noting that inspectors are likely to compare the progress of disadvantaged pupils with all non-disadvantaged pupils, not just with those who have similar starting points because if inspectors only compared the progress and attainment of pupils who started at a similar level, they would be unable to establish if gaps in attainment between disadvantaged and non-disadvantaged pupils were closing.

Inspectors will check that the reason the gap is narrowing is because the attainment and progress of disadvantaged pupils is rising, rather than that of non-disadvantaged pupils falling. If an attainment gap exists or widens, inspectors will also consider whether this is because disadvantaged pupils attain more highly than others do nationally, but non-disadvantaged pupils in the school attain even more highly. The Common Inspection Framework says "these circumstances would not reflect negatively on the school".

Pupil Premium - key questions for Key Stage 3 leaders

In light of all this, I would recommend that leaders of Key Stage 3 prepare for any inspection or DfE visit by asking themselves the following questions:

1. Did I focus sufficiently on literacy and numeracy interventions?
2. Did I work with primary feeders to identify pupils who might benefit from summer schools, nurture groups, etc.?
3. Did I target my best teachers at my most disadvantaged pupils?
4. Did I apply for top-up summer school funding when it was available? (It was removed in 2016.)
5. Do all my teachers know who was eligible for Pupil Premium funding? Do they and governors know how that funding was used and what impact it has had?
6. Where do pupils do their homework and independent study? If they live in chaotic homes, do we provide a quiet space with support? Have I involved parents in making sure pupils use it?
7. What happened after I looked at the data? What interventions did it lead to and what was their impact? What have I learnt?
8. Did I have gaps between exclusion and attendance rates as well as attainment gaps?

9. Was a senior leader at my school responsible for Pupil Premium funding? Do we also have a governor responsible for it?
10. Did higher (and lower) attaining pupils make as much progress as non-FSM? (Remember, the Pupil Premium is not just there to get pupils up to age related minimum expectations.)
11. What did I use as a benchmark when I compared our performance to other schools? (Don't just compare FSM pupils to other FSM pupils; and look beyond LA figures to national standards.)
12. How did I evaluate pastoral interventions? Did I ensure that, ultimately, they led to academic improvements as well as improvements in, say, attendance and behaviour?
13. When did I review my interventions? Did I track, review and improve our provision as I went along rather than wait until the end?

The answers to these questions can provide the basis for your Pupil Premium action plan. So ask yourself: What do you need to do now in order to be fully prepared for inspection?

Above all, as you prepare for inspection, remember this mantra: know thy impact!

Pupil Premium: Good practice

As you start working towards your action plan, what should you be aiming for? What's your end goal? What does good practice in this area look like?

Schools that use the Pupil Premium funding effectively at Key Stage 3 and close the gap tend to conduct a detailed analysis of where pupils are underachieving and why. They make good use of research evidence when choosing support and intervention activities but are discerning customers of research - they always contextualise the information, asking: How would this work in my school? And: What do I know already works in my context?   Research is extremely valuable as a starting point but you must not underestimate your own knowledge of your school and its pupils and staff.

As well as applying research and personal knowledge, schools that use the Pupil Premium funding effectively at Key Stage 3 focus on high quality teaching rather than relying on interventions to compensate because they know that pedagogy trumps all - getting it right first time is the best approach and teaching matters more than curriculum.   They ensure that their best teachers lead English and maths intervention groups.   They make frequent use of achievement data in order to check the effectiveness of interventions and they do this early and continue to do it throughout the year rather than waiting until the intervention has finished and it's too late to change it.

These schools also tend to have a systematic focus on clear pupil feedback and pupils receive regular advice to help them improve their work.   These schools have a designated senior leader with a clear overview of the funding allocation and a solid understanding of how the funding works and how it needs reporting.   All the teachers in these schools are aware of the pupils who are eligible for Pupil Premium funding and they take responsibility for those pupils' progress.   These schools have strategies in place for improving attendance, behaviour and links with families and communities if these are an issue, as well as for improving academic performance.   And, finally, these schools ensure that the performance management of staff includes discussions about the Pupil Premium and about individual pupils in receipt of the funding and how they are progressing.

Pupil Premium: Bad practice

Conversely, in schools where the Pupil Premium isn't used effectively and is not tracked well enough, there tends to be a lack of clarity about the intended impact of interventions.   These schools run the same intervention strategies year after year because that's just what they're used to doing or have the staff and resources for, irrespective of whether or not they work. There is no real monitoring of the quality and impact of the interventions and no real awareness of what works and what offers the best value for money. These schools also tend to spend the money indiscriminately on teaching assistants but TAs are not well utilised.

The schools whose Pupil Premium practice is ineffective also tend to have an unclear audit trail and focus solely on pupils attaining the Level 4 benchmarks not higher. They tend to spend the Pupil Premium in isolation, it does not feature as part of the whole school development plan and decisions about it are not therefore taken in the round. These schools also compare their performance to local, not national, data. Pupil Premium funding is used for pastoral interventions but they are vague and not focused on desired outcomes for pupils. And, finally, in these schools, governors are not involved in taking decisions about Pupil Premium spending and are not informed about its use and impact.

Pupil Premium: What to report

Schools need to report on how much Pupil Premium funding they received in the current academic year and how they intend to spend the funding. They need to be able to articulate their reasons and evidence for this. Schools also need to report on how they spent the funding they received for the last academic year and what difference it made to the attainment of disadvantaged pupils.

The funding is allocated for each financial year, but the information schools publish online should refer to the academic year as this is how parents and the general public understand the school year. As schools won't know how much funding they're getting for the latter part of the academic year (from April to July), they should report on the funding up to the end of the financial year then update the information when they have all the data.

If the school receives Year 7 literacy and numeracy catch-up premium funding, they must also publish details of how they spend this funding and the effect this has had on the attainment of the pupils who attract it.

In Chapter Eleven of this book we will examine ways of making Key Stage 3 literacy and numeracy across the curriculum more effective.

CHAPTER ELEVEN

Literacy and numeracy

Literacy

Many schools already have a clear focus on literacy; it is numeracy that needs to be given greater priority and focus. But there is always room for improvement where literacy is concerned and there can be no issue more critical for schools to resolve...

Indeed, as Ofsted said in their 2012 report 'Moving English Forward', "There can be no more important subject than English in the school curriculum." The report went on to say:

> "English is a pre-eminent world language, it is at the heart of our culture and it is the language medium in which most of our pupils think and communicate. Literacy skills are also crucial to pupils' learning in other subjects across the curriculum."

Literacy is critical to schools because, as a European Union report explained in 2012, "If smart growth is about knowledge and innovation, investment in literacy skills is a prerequisite for achieving such growth." The report added:

"Our world is dominated by the written word, both online and in print. This means we can only contribute and participate actively if we can read and write sufficiently well. But, each year, hundreds of thousands of children start their secondary school two years behind in reading; some leave even further behind their peers... Literacy is about people's ability to function in society as private individuals, active citizens, employees or parents... Literacy is about people's self-esteem, their interaction with others, their health and employability. Ultimately, literacy is about whether a society is fit for the future."

Moreover, in 2010 the National Literacy Trust published a report called 'Literacy: State of the Nation, A Picture of Literacy in the UK Today' in which it reported that 92% of the British public considered literacy to be vital to the economy and essential to getting a good job.

The Ofsted report 'Removing Barriers to Literacy' (2011) concludes that "teachers in a secondary school need to understand that literacy is a key issue regardless of the subject taught". The report goes on to say that literacy is an important element of teachers' effectiveness and that literacy supports learning because "pupils need vocabulary, expression and organisational control to cope with the cognitive demands of all subjects". It also argues that writing helps pupils to "sustain and order thought", that "better literacy leads to improved self-esteem, motivation and behaviour", and that literacy "allows pupils to learn independently" and is therefore "empowering". Moreover, it argues that "better literacy raises pupils' attainment in all subjects".

In 'Outstanding Literacy: A Teacher's Guide to Literacy Across the Curriculum' (2014), Matilda Rose argues: "Every teacher is a teacher of literacy. As a teacher of, say, Science, you have a responsibility to help your pupils learn about science, but you also have a responsibility to help them speak, read and write like a scientist ... It means having an analytical self-awareness, which enables you to identify how you speak, read and write about science ... And this is best done by explaining, demonstrating, modelling, teaching, and giving feedback."

So, although literacy may assume a higher priority than numeracy, there is definitely still room for improvement. As such, I think it worth spending a moment exploring what effective literacy across the curriculum looks like in practice.

According to Slavin & Lake (2008), many effective literacy interventions have cooperative learning at their core and we have already explored metacognition in some detail so I shall not do so again here. However, Brook (2002) identified three key elements of effective teaching approaches that are particularly effective for low attainers in literacy: Early intervention; one-to-one and small group support; and personalisation.

Early intervention, in particular, is critical if we are avoid widening the literacy gap at Key Stage 3. This speaks to the Matthew Effect. Allow me to explain...

Vocabulary is critical to success in reading as well as academic achievement more generally. The size of a pupil's vocabulary in their early years of schooling (the number and variety of words that the young person knows) is a significant predictor of reading comprehension in later schooling and in life. Most children are experienced speakers of the language when they begin school but reading the language requires more complex, abstract vocabulary than that used in everyday conversation. Children who have had stories read to them during the first years of their lives are exposed to a much broader and richer vocabulary than those contained in everyday conversations and, as such, arrive at school better prepared for reading.

In 'Outstanding Literacy', Matilda Rose explains that:

> "Learning vocabulary is an incremental process. Our understanding of a word grows with repeated exposure to it.

Dale & O'Rourke (1986) say that learning vocabulary takes place on a continuum, ranging from never having seen or heard a word before to having a deep knowledge of that word and its different meanings, as well as the ability to use that word confidently and accurately in both speaking and writing. Acquiring vocabulary is incremental because words differ in many ways: they differ according to syntax – knowing what part of speech a particular word is can assist reading; they differ according to the size of their 'family' – knowing one of a family of words will help the reader determine a number of others; some words are polysemous which means they can have multiple meanings (e.g. the word 'scale' means to climb, a feature of a fish, a plant disease, a measuring instrument, the ratio of distance on a map to that on the ground, and much more. Students who know multiple meanings of words are more prepared to read widely and across multiple contexts.

"In short, vocabulary is complex but also vital to developing reading comprehension. If a student knows the meaning of the word happy, and knows the single letter-sounds that make that word, then the word can be easily decoded and understood when read in a text. The words happier and happiness are also more likely to be read and understood. With only a few exposures, these words will be familiar enough to be recognised on sight and so a student's reading vocabulary grows.

"Young people who develop reading skills early in their lives by reading regularly add to their vocabularies exponentially over time. This is sometimes called 'The Matthew Effect' after the line in the Bible (Matthew 13:12), 'The rich shall get richer and the poor shall get poorer'. In the context of literacy, the Matthew Effect is that 'the word rich get richer while the word poor get poorer'."

Daniel Rigney explains this principle further in his book 'The Matthew Effect' (2010): "While good readers gain new skills very rapidly, and quickly move from learning to read to reading to learn, poor readers become increasingly frustrated with the act of reading, and try to avoid reading where possible. Students who begin with high verbal aptitudes find themselves in verbally enriched social environments and have a double advantage. Good readers may choose friends who also read avidly while poor readers seek friends with whom they share other enjoyments."

E D Hirsch, meanwhile, in his book 'The Schools We Need' (1996), says that "The children who possess intellectual capital when they first arrive at school have the mental scaffolding and Velcro to catch hold of what is going on, and they can turn the new knowledge into still more Velcro to gain still more knowledge".

Department for Education research suggests that, by the age of seven, the gap in the vocabulary known by children in the top and bottom quartiles is something like 4,000 words (children in the top quartile know around 7,000 words). The word poor cannot catch up with the word rich because to do so they'd need to be able to learn more words more quickly than the word rich. A pupil who does not know the meaning of the word happy will struggle over that and related words (e.g. happiness, happier, happiest, unhappy) in connected text, even if she can decode them, because transforming letters into words is useless if those words do not have a meaning.

If a pupil continues to experience frustration when reading because she is word poor, then she is likely to give up, denying herself the opportunity to build vocabulary, fluency and world knowledge. Young people who do not acquire these skills easily will become increasingly disadvantaged over time. Vocabulary helps to build comprehension and is therefore a key tool for reading comprehension. Young people who lack vocabulary and prior knowledge (context) will have difficulty understanding the books they encounter in school, especially as those books become more difficult.

It is vital, therefore, that literacy support and interventions - such as one-to-one and small group tuition - are put in place at the very start of Key Stage 3 and not delayed until Key Stage 4 when it will already be too late.

What else can we do in Key Stage 3 to help develop pupils' literacy skills?

Literacy needs to be interwoven into the fabric of everyday school life and involve all staff. It should feature in all the school's development plans and be visible around the school. Literacy should also be a part of all meeting agenda and be regularly discussed at all levels. It always helps if there is a senior leader with literacy and pedagogy knowledge who champions literacy across the curriculum.

A school also needs an effective assessment system which sets literacy targets from national rather than local data. Literacy needs to be taught within a meaningful and relevant curriculum and this might involve the use of a quality phonics programme. Pupils identified as being 'at risk' for literacy should also have a nominated learning mentor. Schools need to develop good partnerships with parents, particularly for pupils who have high needs.

In the classroom, teachers need to allow time for pupils to share and recommend books. It helps if the school recruits influential readers, perhaps older pupils, teachers or volunteers. Local sportspeople are always keen to get involved and act as positive role models. The school should develop and maintain a calendar of reading events to which all departments contribute. All departments should give pupils literacy-targeted rewards such as book vouchers. Teachers of all subjects need to explicitly teach reading skills such as scanning, skimming, and reading for details when relevant to the assignment being set rather than expecting pupils to employ these skills independently and as if through a process of osmosis.

Teachers of all subjects should use Directed Activities Related to Texts (DARTs) to help pupils make sense of a text. For example, cloze (where words are missing from a text and pupils have to fill in the gaps), text marking, sequencing, and text reconstruction are all useful strategies.

Teachers need to engage pupils by linking what they are reading to the world beyond the classroom. They can also vary the way texts are read and by whom the texts are read.

Teachers need to give pupils a real audience, context and purpose for any writing tasks they set and should, where possible, give pupils an opportunity to embed the use of technology - such as blogs and social media - into their writing.

Literacy leaders need to teach the knowledge of texts (such as genre, text types, etc) to all their teaching staff in order to enable teachers to know what features to focus on when planning and teaching reading and writing in their subjects.

Teachers of all subjects need to give pupils sufficient time to complete an extended piece of writing. The process of writing should include crafting and editing and pupils need to be explicitly taught how to draft, edit, and redraft work.

The school needs to develop a consistent policy and approach to teaching spelling, punctuation and grammar (SPaG) and teachers of all subjects need to explicitly teach SPaG in context, linked to the form of writing being developed at the time. To make this work in practice, literacy leaders will need to help all their teaching staff develop their own knowledge.

Teachers should use talk and discussion in order to illustrate the application and effect of grammar and they should develop pupils' knowledge of spelling strategies as well as the rules of spelling. Teachers in all subjects should take a consistent approach to marking spelling.

Teachers in all subjects should use a range of formal talk in lessons and should construct or co-construct with pupils the rules for speaking and listening such as turn-taking, making eye contact, active listening, and so on. Teachers need to make sure all pupils contribute to class discussion by prompting and directing them. Finally, all teachers need to model good speaking and listening skills during class discussions.

Numeracy

Numeracy is often regarded as literacy's poor relation, not given the same amount of time, resources and priority as its close cousin.

After years of investment and a war of attrition, most teachers now understand their role in developing pupils' literacy skills because they recognise that English - reading, and writing, and speaking and listening, are the medium through which pupils learn and articulate their learning right across the curriculum. If they are not literate, pupils will not achieve in any subject.

However, many teachers still struggle to understand their role in developing pupils' numeracy skills and fail to see how their subject presents the same opportunities for embedding numeracy as it does for embedding literacy.

Let us first, then, look at what numeracy means in Key Stage 3 and provide some examples of numeracy at play in various subjects.

Numeracy can be meaningfully divided into four categories: 1. handling information; 2. space, shape and measurements; 3. operations and calculations; and 4. numbers.

Handling information is about graphs and charts, comparing sets of data and types of data, processing data, and probability. Within graphs and charts, you might look at pie and bar charts. You might look at interpreting information, you might look at data in lists and tables, and you might look at reading scales. Within comparing sets of data and types of data, you might look at measures of averages, measures of spread, discrete data and continuous data. Within processing data, you might look at decision trees and VENN diagrams. Within probability, you might look at using a probability scale, estimating probability from statistical information, and experimental probability.

Space, shape and measurements is about both space, shape and measure, and solving problems with space, shape and measure. Within measurements, you might look at standard units of measurements for length, mass, capacity, time, temperature, and area and perimeter, and consider both metric and imperial measurements. You might select and use measuring instruments and look at how to interpret numbers and read scales. You might also look at volume. Within shape and space, you might look at coordinates to describe a position. You might look at simple positional language. You might look at symmetry. You might look at 2D and 3D shapes. And you might look at angles. Solving problems with space, shape and measurements might involve selecting and using appropriate skills to solve geographical problems. It might involve using geographical notation and symbols correctly.

Operations and calculations is about addition and subtraction, multiplication and division, number operations, and the effective use of calculators. Within addition and subtraction you might look at knowing plus and minus facts to twenty, at mental methods to one hundred, and at whole numbers to one thousand and beyond. Within multiplication and division you might look at knowing multiply and divide facts to twenty, and remainders and rounding. Within number operations you might look at inverse operations, interrelationships and order of operations. And within the effective use of calculators you might look a calculations with fractions, decimals and percentages, and calculations with negatives.

Numbers (and the use of the number system) is about using numbers, whole numbers, size and order, place value, patterns and sequences, and numbers 'in between' whole numbers. Within using numbers you might look at reading and writing using symbols and labels, at ratio and proportion, at using numbers for measuring and for counting, and for ratio and proportion. Within whole numbers and size and order you might look at comparing and ordering and using number lines. Within place value you might look at zero as a place holder, at money context, at measures and at estimation. Within sequences and patterns you might look at odd and even, at square numbers, at factors and multiples and at prime numbers. And within numbers 'in between' whole numbers you might look at fractions, decimals and percentages.

Numeracy encompasses three sets of skills: 1. reasoning; 2. problem-solving; and 3. decision-making.

Reasoning might involve identifying structures, being systematic, searching for patterns, developing logical thinking, and predicting and checking. ***Problem-solving*** might involve identifying the information needed to carry out a task, breaking down a problem or task into smaller parts, interpreting solutions in context, and making mental estimates to check the reasonableness of an answer. And ***decision-making*** might involve choosing appropriate strategies, identifying relevant information and choosing the right tools and equipment.

In English, numeracy can be developed by using non-fiction texts which include mathematical vocabulary, graphs, charts and tables. In science, pupils will order numbers including decimals, calculate means, and percentages, use negative numbers when taking temperatures, substitute into formulae, rearrange equations, decide which graph to use to represent data, and plot, interpret and predict from graphs. In ICT, pupils will collect and classify data, enter it into data handling software to produce graphs and tables, and interpret and explain the results. When they use computer models and simulations they will draw on their abilities to manipulate numbers and identify patterns and relationships. In art and design and technology, pupils will use measurements and patterns, spatial ideas, the properties of shapes, and symmetry, and use multiplication and ratio to enlarge and reduce the size of objects. In history, geography and RE, pupils will collect data and use measurements of different kinds. They will study maps and use coordinates and ideas of angles, direction, position, scale, and ratio. And they will use timelines similar to number lines.

*

Hopefully, if you were in any doubt, you can already see how numeracy is a whole-school concern and encompasses skills that apply across the curriculum.

So how can we ensure that numeracy is taught effectively throughout the school at Key Stage 3?

At the whole-school level in Key Stage 3, you need to create a positive environment that celebrates numeracy and provides pupils with role models by celebrating the numeracy successes of older pupils. You also need to ensure that planned activities allow pupils to learn and practice their numeracy skills. You should publicly display examples of high quality numeracy work from across the curriculum around the school. And you should ensure that every department adheres to the school's numeracy policy.

Individual departments at Key Stage 3 should provide high quality exemplar materials and display examples of numeracy work within their subject context. Departments should also highlight opportunities for the use of numeracy within their subject and ensure that the learning materials that are presented to pupils match both their capability in the subject and their numerical demands.

Individual teachers of Key Stage 3 classes, meanwhile, should have high expectations of all their pupils and ensure that the numerical content of their lessons is of a high standard. They should encourage pupils to show their numerical working out where relevant and encourage the use of estimation, particularly for checking work. Teachers should also encourage pupils to write mathematically-correct statements and to vocalise their maths. They should also encourage pupils to use non-calculator methods wherever possible. Teachers and departments should inform the maths department as soon as possible if any numeracy problems are identified.

Part Six

Conclusion

CHAPTER TWELVE

Conclusion

In Chapter One I explained that Ofsted's report Key Stage 3: The Wasted Years? found that, while pupils generally had the opportunity to study a broad range of subjects throughout Key Stage 3, in too many schools the quality of teaching and the rate of pupils' progress and achievement were not good enough.

Inspectors reported concerns about the effectiveness of Key Stage 3 in one in five of the routine inspections, particularly in relation to the slow progress made in English and maths and the lack of challenge for the most able pupils. Inspectors also reported significant weaknesses in MFL, history and geography at Key Stage 3. Too often, inspectors found teaching that failed to challenge and engage pupils. Additionally, low-level disruption in some of these lessons, particularly in MFL, had a detrimental impact on the pupils' learning. Achievement was not good enough in just under half of the MFL classes observed, two-fifths of the history classes and one third of the geography classes.

The report claimed that the weaknesses inspectors identified in teaching and pupil progress reflect a general lack of priority given to Key Stage 3 by many secondary school leaders. The majority of leaders spoken to as part of the survey, the report said, admitted they staffed Key Stages 4 and 5 before Key Stage 3. As a result, some Key Stage 3 classes were split between more than one teacher or were taught by non-specialists. In this sense - and in the way schools monitored and assessed pupils' progress - Key Stage 3 was a poor relation to the other key stages.

The report also asserted that too many secondary schools did not work effectively with partner primary schools to understand pupils' prior learning and ensure that they built on this during Key Stage 3. Some secondary leaders simply accepted that pupils would repeat what they had already done in primary school during the early part of Key Stage 3, particularly in Year 7. In addition, half of the pupils surveyed said that their homework never, or only some of the time, helped them to make progress. And inspectors found that, too often, homework did not consolidate or extend pupils' learning.

The report claimed that some school leaders did not use the Pupil Premium effectively in Key Stage 3 to ensure that gaps between disadvantaged pupils and their peers continued to close following transition to secondary school. Instead, additional support tended to be focused on intervention activities at Key Stage 4, which by then would have to compensate for ineffective practice in the earlier years of secondary education.

In summary, the report's key findings are as follows:

- Key Stage 3 is not a high priority for many secondary school leaders in timetabling, assessment and monitoring of pupils' progress. Eighty five per cent of senior leaders interviewed said that they staff Key Stages 4 and 5 before

Key Stage 3. Key Stage 3 is given lower priority, where classes are more often split between more than one teacher or where pupils are taught by non-specialists.

- Leaders prioritise the pastoral over the academic needs of pupils during transition from primary school. While this affects all pupils, it can have a particularly detrimental effect on the progress and engagement of the most able.
- Many secondary schools do not build sufficiently on pupils' prior learning. Many of the senior leaders interviewed said that they do not do this well enough and accepted that some pupils would repeat some of what they had done in Key Stage 2.
- Some school leaders are not using the Pupil Premium funding effectively to close gaps quickly in Key Stage 3. Inspection evidence and senior leaders' comments indicate that this is another area where Key Stage 4 often takes priority.
- Developing pupils' literacy skills in Key Stage 3 is a high priority in many schools but the same level of priority is not evident for numeracy. A majority of the headteachers Ofsted spoke to were able to explain how they were improving literacy at Key Stage 3 but only a quarter could do the same for numeracy. This is reflected in inspection evidence, for example in monitoring inspections inspectors reported improvements in literacy nearly three times more often than they did in numeracy.
- Homework is not consistently providing the opportunities for pupils to consolidate or extend their learning in Key Stage 3. Approximately half of the pupils who responded to Ofsted's online questionnaire said that their homework never, or only some of the time, helps them to make progress.

In concluding their report, Ofsted recommended senior leaders should make Key Stage 3 a higher priority in all aspects of school planning, monitoring and evaluation, and ensure that not only is the curriculum offer at Key

Stage 3 broad and balanced, but that teaching is of high quality and prepares pupils for more challenging subsequent study at Key Stages 4 and 5.

Ofsted also recommended that senior leaders ensure that transition from Key Stage 2 to 3 focuses as much on pupils' academic needs as it does on their pastoral needs, and that senior leaders foster better cross-phase partnerships with primary schools in order to ensure that Key Stage 3 teachers build on pupils' prior knowledge, understanding and skills.

Ofsted said middle and senior leaders should make sure that systems and procedures for assessing and monitoring pupils' progress in Key Stage 3 are more robust and that leaders should focus on the needs of disadvantaged pupils in Key Stage 3, including the most able, in order to close the achievement gap as quickly as possible. Leaders should also evaluate the quality and effectiveness of homework in Key Stage 3 in order to ensure that it helps pupils to make good progress. And finally school leaders should put in place literacy and numeracy strategies that ensure pupils build on their prior attainment in Key Stage 2 in these crucial areas.

In Chapter One I explained that whilst all of Ofsted's recommendations were sensible and worthwhile, they were also - perhaps understandably for a high level report - vague and intangible. For example, what does it mean, in reality, to give Key Stage 3 a high priority? What, in practice, do cross-phase partnerships look like? What is robust assessment and monitoring, exactly? And what, precisely, constitutes quality and effective homework?

Over the course of this book, I have explored these recommendations in greater depth and detail as I have sought to offer my own advice on how to lead an effective Key Stage 3 and ensure that the three-years of a child's education that constitute Key Stage 3 do not prove to be time wasted but are instead fruitful, enjoyable and rewarding. I hope we are now in a position to confidently and robustly answer the question that forms the title of Ofsted's report - KS3: The Wasted Years? - with a firm and frank 'no'.

*

The secret to an effective Key Stage 3, as I have argued, is a better transition process (by which I mean a more effective transition between Key Stages 2 and 3 but also within Key Stage 3 itself as pupils transfer between Years 7, 8 and 9), a better curriculum (by which I mean curriculum continuity between the key stages, a curriculum that is challenging, engaging and different to that which precedes and succeeds it, and provides for the effective development of literacy and numeracy skills), better homework (by which I mean homework that enables pupils to practice their skills and provides a real audience, purpose and context), and better assessment (by which I mean the regular monitoring of progress, quality formative feedback, and timely interventions which seek to close the gaps in the performance of different groups of pupils).

By way of conclusion, let me end with six features of an effective Key Stage 3 transition and induction process, each littered with suggestions for further reading. I am indebted to the Department for Education for many of the reports cited in this chapter.

Feature 1 - Collaborate before and after pupils transfer from primary school

Research shows that collaboration between primary and secondary schools both before and after pupils transfer from Year 6 into Year 7 is an important feature of a smooth and effective transition process. The Department for Education (then called the Department for Children, Schools and Families) carried out research in 2008 across seven local authorities involving forty-seven primary and secondary schools (including some special schools) in order to explore what could strengthen their transfer and transition practices. The final report concluded that effective transfer did not involve one key stage 'doing' transfer to the next, but an equal partnership that had professionally developed all stakeholders.

Likewise, Galton et al. (1999, 2003) highlighted the importance of Year 6 and Year 7 teachers working together to plan and teach "bridging units" (projects which were started towards the end of Year 6 and completed at the start of Year 7) in order to help inform and personalise the pupil transfer experience.

Other examples of effective collaboration might include the establishment of cross-phase working processes both within and between children's services. It might include planning schemes of work that promote curriculum continuity and a consistency of teaching and learning styles. It might include the facilitation and support of local cross-phase networking meetings of families of schools to jointly plan for strengthening transfer and the joint working between teachers in different key stages to promote an understanding of pupils' abilities and levels of knowledge. Galton suggests work on planning and teaching bridging units should be jointly planned to maximise personalisation.

Feature 2 - Communicate effectively between the phases and with pupils/parents

Effective communication between teachers from different school/phases, and with parents/carers and pupils is key to improving the transition from primary to secondary school.

Effective communication between teachers from different school phases can be achieved by arranging regular visits by secondary teachers to primary school and, in return, visits by primary teachers to secondary school. These visits can take many forms including:

Talks to pupils in assemblies and form time about their respective schools; taster lessons, especially opportunities for pupils to experience secondary school facilities such as science labs and design and technology workshops; teachers working together to plan lessons and discuss curriculum design, as well as observe each other in the classroom; teachers organising CPD sessions and teaching and learning conferences together, as well as professional dialogue and the dissemination of research findings and materials, and the sharing of good practice.

Effective communication with parents can be achieved by involving parents in a school's preparation for transition and by developing their understanding of the culture of the new school, helping them understand what to expect. In practice, this might include promoting and enhancing the role of parent/carer partnerships such as through the use parent/carer advisers as explained by Greenhough et al. in their 2007 paper and by the DCSF in 2008. It can also be achieved through the use of parent voice mechanisms which gather, monitor and evaluate parental views in relation to transfers and transitions and give feedback and updates to parents showing how the school has listened to and responded to parents' questions and concerns.

Effective communication with pupils can be achieved by providing information about what to expect at each stage of the transfer process and where and who to go to for help or to have questions answered, as explained by Sanders et al (2005). It can also be achieved by ensuring that pupils are involved in the transition process at all stages, and are well informed of what to expect in their new school, as outlined by Schulting et al. (2005) and LoCasale-Crouch et al. (2008).

Feature 3 - School visits and induction programmes should be given priority

School visits and induction programmes can improve social and academic outcomes if they are given priority and invested in. In other words, to be effective, they need to be well-planned and appropriately resourced and staffed.

School visits work best when they are planned and publicised long before pupils transfer in order to give pupils and their parents/carers a good understanding of the new school and its systems and structures, expectations and routines. Induction programmes also work best when the teachers involved are provided with appropriate training and detailed information about what they're expected to achieve. The induction also needs to be well structured and engaging with high quality resources. The planning and teaching of induction programmes needs to involve the core subjects of English, maths and science. Ideally, prior to induction and as part of the school visits, pupils in primary schools should be enabled to make regular use of secondary school facilities in order to become familiar with secondary teachers, buildings and methods. Where daytime visits by primary pupils is not possible, after school clubs run by secondary teachers for pupils from their feeder primaries is a useful means of encouraging future pupils to become familiar with their new school prior to transfer.

Feature 4 - Differentiate the transition experience for all pupils

Different types of pupils experience the transfer and transition process in different ways. As such, they require different types of support and at different stages of the process. In practice, this might take the form of identifying vulnerable pupils and assigning a dedicated teaching assistant to them to provide additional guidance and skills development. It might mean modifying the process for pupils with special educational needs and disabilities (SEND), consulting educational psychologists, for example, about the emotional impact of life changes on vulnerable young people. It might mean establishing dedicated summer schools for those pupils who are identified as at risk of falling behind at the start of the new academic year and continuing to work with them to ensure the gap does not widen in the intervening weeks between the end of Year 6 and the beginning of Year 7. For more, see Taverner et al. (2001).

Feature 5 - Senior leaders need to support transition and all staff need clearly defined roles and responsibilities

A smooth and successful transition process depends on the whole school coming together, working effectively as one in the interests of pupils' social, emotional and academic success. To achieve this, all school staff need clearly defined roles and responsibilities, and senior staff need to provide effective leadership for transition which means being engaged in all aspects of the process.

In practice, this means that the headteacher and senior leadership team have to provide their full support for the transition process - financially, in terms of resources, and psychologically. There needs to be a designated senior leader responsible for transition with the status to give it importance and able to align these processes with wider school improvement priorities.

This also means that all other school staff have clearly defined responsibilities for transition. For example, there will be a member of staff who is the school's named person responsible for meeting parents/carers who want to drop in and discuss issues. They will be another member of staff responsible for managing data on new pupils (including prior attainment at Key Stages 1 and 2, and teacher assessments). And there will be a member of staff responsible for listening and responding to pastoral issues amongst new pupils.

In terms of senior leaders 'putting their money where their mouths are' by allocating appropriate resources to enable a smooth and successful transition, this might mean timetabling experienced teachers in Year 7 and, where possible, making teaching assistants available to provide in-class support for the first half term immediately following transfer. TAs are particularly useful because they can contribute to assessment, support pupils with SEND, provide valuable insights into the needs of individual pupils and maintain established routines when they change classes with individual pupils.

Senior leaders can also play a vital role in ensuring that high quality data is available for every pupil joining a new school, and in establishing a clear strategic vision for strengthening transfers and transitions through the work of the governing body, self-evaluation and the school improvement plan. Senior leaders and other staff with responsibility for transition can aid the transition process by developing a transfer and transitions policy that aligns with the school improvement plan and contributes to raising standards and closing attainment gaps between identified groups. And, finally, they can engage with and contribute to local and national plans to share effective practice and develop consistency. Talking of sharing best practice...

Feature 6 - Share best practice

The transfer and transition process can be further improved if examples of good practice are identified and disseminated. For example, schools could engage with local and national research evidence about various aspects of transfer. Senior leaders, teachers and other adults who work with pupils and/or their families could engage in professional development activities including action research. And groups of schools could work together to build leadership capacity and develop a greater knowledge base by involving pupils and parents/carers in the monitoring, reviewing and planning process, and by strategically sharing effective practice.

Postscript - More testing is not the answer

Above I share, by way of conclusion, six features of an effective transition and induction process which will improve pupils' motivation and progress in Key Stage 3, thus ensuring that those three years of a child's education are not wasted but are fruitful and rewarding.

Just prior to the publication of this book, the Chief Inspector suggested another potential solution to the problem of Key Stage 3: more testing. It's safe to say, however, that judging by the response he garnered from teachers, school leaders and professional associations, he was somewhat wide of the mark...

In fact, the headline on the BBC News website which reported the HMCI's comments ran: "Introducing yet more testing of students is "not the answer" to ensuring the most-able pupils achieve their potential."

The Chief Inspector, Sir Michael Wilshaw, who - at the time - was in the dying days of his tenure as the head of Ofsted and, one might argue, keen to hog the headlines with polemics before retiring, called for the return of SATs at age 14.

Key Stage 3 SATs were scrapped in 2008, but Sir Michael said that he believes the decision was a mistake. He based his opinion on the fact that Ofsted had previously reported that thousands of pupils who achieved well at primary school failed to reach their "full potential" at secondary level – especially those from disadvantaged backgrounds.

Sir Michael said that this was often down to poor transition arrangements, which left gifted pupils "treading water in their first few years of secondary". He also blamed low expectations and insufficient checks to ensure teaching stretched the most able in mixed ability classrooms.

He went on to say:

> "The most recent statistics paint a bleak picture of under-achievement and unfulfilled potential. Thousands of our most able secondary-age children are still not doing as well as they should in the non-selective state sector where the vast majority of them are educated.
>
> "Last year, 68 per cent of non-selective secondary school pupils who had achieved a Level 5 or above in both English and mathematics at the end of primary school failed to attain A* or A grades in these subjects at GCSE.
>
> "Indeed, 27 per cent of previously high-attaining pupils failed to even achieve the minimum expected progress – a grade B in both these key subjects at GCSE.
>
> "What is most depressing is that the brightest children from disadvantaged backgrounds are the most likely not to achieve their full potential. The most able children in receipt of Pupil Premium funding still lag well behind their more advantaged peers. They are also less likely to be entered for the English Baccalaureate than other bright pupils and when they are entered, are less likely to achieve it."

And his solution? Sir Michael argued that the introduction of harder Key Stage 1 and 2 tests had contributed to narrowing the gap for Pupil Premium pupils at primary level and, therefore, he believes the same could happen at Key Stage 3.

He said:

> "It is a national scandal that the 28 percentage point gap between free school meal and non-FSM pupils at age 16 has barely shifted in 10 years. I believe that one of the principal reasons for this gap at secondary school is the absence of any formal testing between the ages of 11 and 16. This means that many bright children, especially from poorer homes, are allowed to drift through their first few years of secondary school. Their progress and early promise are stifled from this point onwards.
>
> "I urge the government to consider bringing back external national testing at Key Stage 3. I firmly believe that it was a

mistake to abolish these tests in the first place. If we are serious about helping all disadvantaged children, but especially the most able, to learn well and unlock their full potential, we need to know how they are doing at 14 as well as at seven, 11 and 16."

However, Sir Michael's solution to the problem of Key Stage 3 'the wasted years' was not shared by the teaching profession...

Both the National Association of Head Teachers and the Association of School and College Leaders, for example, warned that more testing was not the answer...

NAHT general secretary Russell Hobby said: "At a time when the government is struggling to manage SATs at Key Stage 1 and Key Stage 2, it would be disastrous to reintroduce SATs for Key Stage 3. The system cannot cope with yet more tinkering, and the government has to ask the question what assessment is actually for."

His counterpart at ASCL, Malcolm Trobe, added: "Subjecting children to even more testing and schools to even more sanctions is not a panacea to every challenge. The amount of formal testing is already onerous and the accountability system is fearsome. These top-down 'solutions' have been tried too often over complex issues which require a more sophisticated approach."

I have to agree: more testing is not the answer to the problem of Key Stage 3. Weighing the pig, as the cliche goes, does not make it fatter. Rather, we need to nurture our porcine stock with the richest of diets.

The answer is not more high-stakes testing which will demoralise pupils further and replicate the conditions of Key Stage 4; rather, the answer - as I've argued throughout this book - is:

1. To improve the transition process - by which I mean ensure there is a more effective transfer between Key Stages 2 and 3 but also a more

effective transition within Key Stage 3 itself as pupils transfer between Years 7, 8 and 9)

2. To improve the Key Stage 3 curriculum - by which I mean ensure there is a greater level of curriculum continuity between Key Stages 2 and 3, and the curriculum in Years 7, 8 and 9 is challenging, engaging and different to that which precedes and succeeds it, and also provides for the effective development of literacy and numeracy skills

3. To improve the quality and effectiveness of homework - by which I mean ensure that homework in Key Stage 3 enables pupils to practice their skills, and that tasks provide a real audience, purpose and context,

4. To improve the quality and effectiveness of assessment - by which I mean ensure there is regular monitoring of progress, quality formative feedback, and timely interventions in place for every pupil throughout Years 7, 8 and 9 which seek to close the gaps in the performance of different groups of pupils.

End Matter

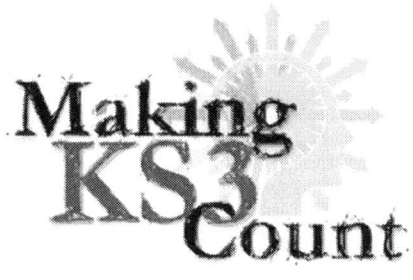

Bibliography

Belenky, DM, Nokes-Malach, TJ (2012), Motivation and Transfer: The role of mastery-approach goals in preparation for future learning. Journal of the Learning Sciences, 21(3), pp 399-432

Bennet, S, Kalish, N (2006), The Case Against Homework: How homework is hurting our children and what we can do about it. Crown. New York.

Biggs, JB, Rihn, BA (1984), The Effects of Intervention on Deep and Surface Approaches to Learning. In Kirby, JR (ED), Cognitive Strategies and Educational Performance (pp 279-293). Academic Press. Orlando.

Centre for Excellence and Outcomes in Children and Young People's Services, (2010), Effective Classroom Strategies for Closing the Gap in Educational Achievement for Children and Young People Living in Poverty, Including White Working Class Boys.

DCSF (2008), What Makes a Successful Transition to Secondary School?

DCSF (2009), Improving Reading: A Handbook for Improving Reading in Key Stages 3 and 4

DCSF (2009), Improving Writing: A Handbook for KS3

DCSF (2009), Narrowing the Gaps: From data analysis to impact: the golden thread

DfE (2011), How do Pupils Progress in Key Stages 2 and 3?

DfE (2012), Encouraging Reading for Pleasure: What the research says on reading for pleasure

DfES (2004), Transition and Progression Within Key Stage 3.

Education Standards Research Team (2012), Research Evidence on Reading on Pleasure

Galton, M (1999), The Impact of School Transitions and Transfer on Pupil Progress and Attainment. Cambridge for DfEE.

Galton, M (2002), Research for Teachers: Transfer from the Primary Classroom. (www.tla.ac.uk)

GSR (2011), Investigating the Drop in Attainment During the Transition Phase With a Particular Focus on Child Poverty. (www.dera.ioe.ac.uk)

Hattie, J (2009), Visible Learning. Routledge. London.

Hattie, J (2012), Visible Learning for Teachers. Routledge. London.

Keith, TZ (1982), Time Spent on Homework and High School Grades: A large sample path analysis. Journal of Educational Psychology, 74, pp 248-253.

Mannion, J, Mercer, N, (2016), Learning to Learn: Improving attainment, closing the gap at Key Stage 3. The Curriculum Journal, 27:2, pp 246-271.

Marzano, RJ, Pickering, DJ (2007), Special Topic: The case for and against homework. Educational Leadership,

64(6), pp 74-79.

McGee, Mizelle (2004), Transition to Secondary School: A literature review. (www.researchgate.net)

National College for Teaching and Leadership (2013), Closing the Gap: How system leaders and schools can work together

National College for School Leadership / Curee (2010), Leadership for Closing the Gap.

National Literacy Trust (2012), Literacy: State of the Nation

National Literacy Trust (2014), Literacy Guide for Secondary Schools

National Numeracy (2013), Essentials of Numeracy. (www.nationalnumeracy.org.uk)

NFER (2006), Transition from Primary to Secondary School: Current arrangements and good practice in Wales. (www.nfer.ac.uk)

Ofsted (2002), Changing Schools: Effectiveness of transfer arrangements at age 11.

Ofsted (2009), English at a Crossroads

Ofsted (2011), Excellence in English

Ofsted (2011), Removing Barriers to English

Ofsted (2012), Moving English Forward

Ofsted (2013), Improving Literacy in Secondary Schools: A Shared Responsibility

Ofsted (2015), Key Stage 3: The wasted years?

Palinscar and Brown (1982), Recriprocal Teaching of Comprehension – Fostering and Comprehension – Monitoring Activities; Cognition and Instruction, I (2), pp 117-175

Palmer, S (2001), How to Teach Writing Across the Curriculum. Ages 8-14 (A Writer's Workshop) 2nd Edition. Routledge. London.

Paschal, RA, Weinstein, T, Walberg, HJ (1984), The Effects of Homework on Learning: A quantitative synthesis. Journal of Educational Research, 78(2), pp97-104.

Perkins, DN, Saloman, G (2012, Knowledge to Go: A motivational and dispositional view of transfer. Educational Psychologist, 47(3), pp248-258).

Pintrich, P, de Groot, E (1990), Motivational and Self-Regulated Learning Components of Classroom Academic Performance. Journal of Educational Psychology, 82, pp 33-40.

Robinson, V, Hohepa, M, Lloyd, C, (2009), School Leadership and Student Outcomes: Identifying what works and why (BES). Ministry of Education. Wellington, NZ.

Schagen, S, Kerr, D (1999), Bridging the Gap? The national curriculum and progression from primary to secondary school. National Foundation for Educational Research for DfEE.

Slavin, RE, (2010), Cooperative Learning: What Makes Groupwork Work? In Dumont, H, Istance D, Benavides, F (Ed), The Nature of Learning: Using research to inspire practice (pp161 – 178). OECD. Paris.

Sutton Trust/EEF (2015), Toolkit of Strategies to Improve Learning: Summary for schools spending the Pupil Premium.

Timperley, H, Wilson, A, Barrar, H, Fung, I, (2007), Teacher Professional Learning and Development: Best Evidence Synthesis Iteration (BES). Ministry of Education. Wellington, NZ.

Vatterott, C (2010), Five Hallmarks of Good Homework. Educational Leadership, 68(1), pp10-15.

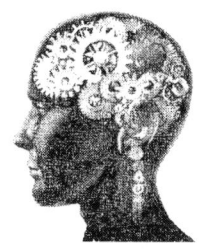

THE IQ MYTH

M J Bromley

www.booksforschool.eu

AUTUS BOOKS
England, UK
www.booksforschool.eu
Twitter: @AutusBooks

First Published in 2012

Original ISBN-13: **978-1478334255**
Original ISBN-10: **1478334258**

For all my former students

THE IQ MYTH

Contents

Making Key Stage 3 Count

"A few modern philosophers assert that an individual's intelligence is a fixed quantity, a quantity which cannot be increased. We must protest and react against this brutal pessimism... with practice, training, and above all, method, we manage to increase our attention, our memory, our judgment and literally to become more intelligent than we were before."

– Alfred Binet, inventor of the IQ test

CHAPTER ONE

Teachers not judges

We are teachers. We are paid to teach our students how: how to broaden their experiences; how to expand their knowledge; how to develop their skills.

We are not judges. We are not paid to sit in judgment about our students' abilities and intellect, nor to make life-changing decisions about what our students are and are not capable of doing.

And yet many teachers do just this: they act like judges. They say things like, "He hasn't got the ability to study my subject" or "She's not bright enough to get a C," or - even worse, "He'll never be a doctor because he's not intelligent enough". Any teacher who places barriers in the way of his or her students in this manner is, in my opinion, a very poor teacher indeed.

After all, what is intelligence?

I suppose the most common measure of someone's intelligence is the IQ test. And yet this test was devised by the Parisian Alfred Binet at the start of the twentieth century - not as a measure of innate intellect or ability, nor as a number which could be used to determine what someone was and was not capable of - but as a way of identifying children who were not profiting from the Paris public school system. Binet used the IQ test to help him design new - by which is meant 'more effective' - educational programmes to help get Parisian schoolchildren back on track.

Let's take a moment to think about that... the IQ test was devised in order to identify students who needed help to improve. The IQ test was devised in order to identify a better school system for these children. It was a snapshot of what these students could do at that moment in time - a measure of current performance, if you like - designed to identify students who were being failed by the school system. In other words, it did not show someone's intellect, it showed whether or not the school system was working for them.

So Binet (without explicitly denying that there were differences in children's intellects) believed that education and practice could bring about fundamental changes in intelligence. Binet said, in his book 'Major Ideas About Children', that "a few modern philosophers assert that an individual's intelligence is a fixed quantity, a quantity which cannot be increased. We must protest and react against this brutal pessimism...with practice, training, and above all, method, we manage to increase our attention, our memory, our judgment and literally to become more intelligent than we were before."

CHAPTER TWO

Practice, training and method

Practice, training, and above all, method - Binet's words. These three things - uttered over a hundred years ago - are still a perfect summary of what the best teachers provide for their students. The best teachers do not sit in judgment; the best teachers provide a safe and secure environment in which all students can learn without fear of failure and in which all students can increase their intelligence with practice.

The Stanford University psychologist, Dr Carol S. Dweck, said in her book, 'Mindset': "Today most experts agree that it's not either-or. It's not nature or nurture, genes or environment. From conception on, there's a constant give and take between the two.... People may start with different temperaments and different aptitudes, but it is clear that experience, training and personal effort take them the rest of the way".

Their choice of words may differ slightly but their sentiment is the same - Dweck and Binet agree that everyone can improve with practice; they agree that effort is more important than 'talent' or 'innate ability'.

This is an important lesson for every teacher to learn. Teachers must challenge their students to be the best, they should not teach to the 'lowest common denominator'. They must have high expectations of all their students and they must encourage their students to take a leap of faith even if that means falling over a few times.

I'd go even further than this: teachers must actively encourage their students to make mistakes, they must foster a safe and secure environment in which falling over is not only accepted without criticism or humiliation, but it is actively encouraged as evidence of effective learning and of getting better at something.

Every teacher knows that some students do not raise their hands in class to answer a question because they fear they will be criticised or made to feel embarrassed for being wrong. And yet the opposite should be true: students should be eager to raise their hands because to get an answer wrong is to learn from their mistake; to get an answer wrong is to find out the correct answer. Equally, raising a hand to say, 'I don't understand this...can you help?' is not a sign of weakness or low intelligence, it is a means of increasing one's intelligence.

Schools are seats of learning, therefore students must be encouraged to learn. This means that teachers must encourage purposeful practice not stifle it by creating the impression that making mistakes is failing, that getting something wrong is a sign of low intelligence.

Of course, making a mistake - even if you have a positive mindset - can be a painful experience. But a mistake shouldn't define you; it's a problem to be faced and learnt from.

CHAPTER THREE

Reap what you sow

Teachers' attitudes directly affect their students' learning and, ultimately, the grades they get. A teacher who has high expectations of every student in his or her class will reap the rewards: their students will rise to the challenge and they will succeed. A teacher who 'dumbs down' and expects students to make little or no progress will get just that in return: 'dumb' students who make little or no progress. I have seen it in practice time and again: teachers who set challenging, aspirational targets and push their students to be the best that they can be, teachers who create an atmosphere in which students truly believe they can make progress and exceed others' expectations, get results; teachers who 'teach to the lowest common denominator' quite simply don't.

I once shared a GCSE English class - a Set 2 according to my timetable - with another teacher. In my first lesson at the start of Year 10, I told the class to ignore the targets they had been given (these being Bs and Cs) and instead to strive to be the best they can be, to aim for the top: A grades. I only ever shared the assessment objectives and grade descriptors for A grade work. I told them that nothing stood in the way of them getting As. All that they needed to do was work hard, listen to my advice and believe that they could get better with practice, training and method. Practice meant working hard, acting on feedback; training meant knowing how to succeed, understanding what examiners were looking for and how to 'do exams'; method meant creating the right atmosphere, a safe and secure environment in which making mistakes was a sign of improving one's intelligence and taking risks meant getting better - in short, an environment in which learning how to fall meant learning how to walk.

My colleague, meanwhile, told the class that their targets were too high and that they should be aiming for no higher than C and D grades. He told the class that they weren't intelligent enough to get As and focused his teaching on how they could get Cs instead. He thought he was doing them a good service: he didn't want to raise hopes or give false praise. He didn't want them to feel under too much pressure and hoped that, without high expectations hanging over them, they might surprise him.

But, perhaps unsurprisingly, for me they got As and Bs in their coursework and exams whereas for my colleague they got Cs and Ds. I do not mean to criticise a colleague who I knew to be an excellent English teacher of long-standing, nor do I wish to present myself as an expert - I'm not. But my colleague had a fixed mindset (about which, more later). He believed that test scores told the whole story of a student's ability (and, more worryingly, their capability) rather than simply providing a snapshot of their attainment at that moment in time. He believed that students who had previously got C grades couldn't get higher. Students in a Set 2 would remain there from start to finish. I, on the other hand, believed in my students' capacities to get better; I believed they could achieve higher grades with practice, training, and method.

I was no more skilled a teacher than my colleague, in fact I was less experienced. My colleague produced more detailed lesson plans than I did: his were carefully constructed, mine consisted of a handwritten note in my diary. My colleague's understanding of Shakespeare plays was deeper than my own; I loved (and still love) Shakespeare with a passion my wife finds frankly odd but I couldn't quote as much of the bard's canon as my colleague.

But I knew my students and I knew what motivated them. I threw away the teacher's handbook and used all the finely-tuned weapons in my armoury: sarcasm, more sarcasm and a bit more sarcasm. (Incidentally, the first thing I was told when training to be a teacher was never use sarcasm: what nonsense! There are no hard and fast rules for teaching except 'be yourself, be human'.) I bonded with my students; I made fun of them and they made fun of me. Colleagues walking past my open classroom door may have thought me unprofessional - or worse, may have assumed I couldn't control my class - when they overheard students jokily insulting me and, dare I say it, laughing! But I knew this was how our relationship worked, I knew they respected me and listened to my advice, not because I had told them they had to ('I'm the teacher, show me some respect') but because I'd earned it by proving myself and by respecting them. They were, without exception, an absolute joy to teach and I hope they enjoyed our lessons half as much as I did. The fact some of them still contact me from time to time to tell me what they're up to, to share their latest successes, means more to me than the A grades they were awarded.

In short, I convinced my class that their abilities were not set in stone and that, just because their prior attainment suggested that they should aim for a C grade, that didn't mean they couldn't and shouldn't aim for the top, and with a little hard work - with practice, training and method - that they wouldn't plant their flag at the summit. My colleague taught them that Shakespeare wrote in iambic pentameter; I taught them to believe in themselves, to believe that nothing was impossible. I taught them about the power of learning and I helped them to enjoy learning.

CHAPTER FOUR

Change your mindset

In her book, 'Mindset', Dweck says that believing "your qualities are carved in stone - the fixed mindset - creates an urgency to prove yourself over and over. If you have only a certain amount of intelligence, a certain personality and a certain moral character - well then you'd better prove that you have a healthy dose of them...." A person with a fixed mindset doesn't believe that 'If at first you don't succeed, try and try again', they believe, 'If at first you don't succeed, then give up because you probably don't have the ability'.

Dweck compares this fixed mindset with what she calls the 'growth mindset'. The growth mindset, by contrast, "is based on the belief that your basic qualities are things you can cultivate through your efforts. Although people may differ in every which way - in their initial talents and aptitudes, interests, or temperaments - everyone can change and grow through application and experience."

Dweck goes on: "Do people with [a growth mindset] believe that anyone can be anything, that anyone with proper motivation or education can become Einstein or Beethoven? No, but they believe that a person's true potential is unknown (and unknowable); that it's impossible to foresee what can be accomplished with years of passion, toil, and training."

This belief that one can develop important qualities actually fosters a deeper passion for learning. After all, why waste time proving over and over again just how great you are, when you could be getting better instead? Why hide your deficiencies when you could be overcoming them?

Good learners are acutely aware of their strengths and areas for development. They know what they do well and what they could do better. So, who has the most accurate view of their strengths and areas for development? Is it those with a fixed mindset or those with a growth mindset? Unsurprisingly, Dweck's research found that people with a fixed mindset "greatly misestimated their performance and their ability [whilst] people with the growth mindset were amazingly accurate". Why should this be? Because, as Dweck says, "If, like those with the growth mindset, you believe you can develop yourself, then you're open to accurate information about your current abilities, even if it's unflattering. What's more, if you're oriented towards learning, as they are, you need accurate information about your current abilities in order to learn effectively".

CHAPTER FIVE

Learning how to fall

I have three daughters. My youngest is, at the time of writing, 18 months old. Over the last year and a half I have watched her closely as she has developed and learnt new skills each and every day. And what has struck me most is just how resilient she is. Although my parental bias leads me to believe that she is the most beautiful girl ever to have walked the earth, my mind knows that she is not unique: every child is just as resilient as she.

When she first started walking, she must have fallen over a least ten times an hour. Often she would tumble into something and injure herself. And did she give up? Did she assume she wasn't going to be any good at this walking lark? Did she resign herself to a life of crawling on her hands and knees? Crawling to work, crawling to the pub? Of course not, she persisted; she picked herself up off the floor, dusted herself down, and tried again. Now she's learning to talk and she's doing it all over again: she's making mistakes and stumbling over words and noises. She sometimes forgets that dogs go 'woof' and cats go 'meow' and sometimes calls my wife 'Daddy'. But will she give up and assume she hasn't the talent for speaking? Will she resign herself to life as a mute, pointing at what she wants and crying when she's frustrated or tired? No, she will persevere until she has mastered the English language because this is what we do.

You see, we are each of us born with an intense desire to learn. We want to develop, we want to improve. And young children stretch themselves every day to learn new skills. You may think they have it easy because they are learning simple tasks whilst we have to grapple with more complex notions and ideas, but you'd be wrong: they are learning the most difficult tasks of a lifetime; they are learning fundamentals such as walking and talking. But they never decide it's too hard or not worth the effort, they don't worry about making mistakes or humiliating themselves. They walk, they fall, and they get up and try again.

*

There's another problem with teachers sitting in judgment...to do so is to assume that students are either born with, or without, talent. To judge a student's intelligence and make decisions based on this judgment (e.g. to decide that a student isn't bright enough to study Triple Science at GCSE) is to suggest that a student can not improve his or her performance in time and given practice, training, and method. This is fundamentally wrong because...

CHAPTER SIX

There's no such thing as talent

Malcolm Gladwell, author of 'Outliers', has suggested that as a society we value natural, effortless accomplishments over achievement through effort. We endow our heroes with superhuman abilities that lead them inevitably towards greatness. People with the growth mindset, however, believe something very different. For them, even geniuses have to work hard for their achievements. Anyway, what's heroic, they would say, about having a gift?

Let's look at some examples of so-called genius:

Thomas Edison is credited with inventing the light bulb. But he was not an innate genius who single-handedly, effortlessly discovered his invention in - and forgive the pun - a 'light bulb moment'. He had thirty assistants, including highly-trained scientists, often working around the clock in a corporate-funded state-of-the-art laboratory. 'His' invention was the culmination of a lot of time-consuming work involving mathematicians, chemists, physicists, engineers and glass-blowers. Yes, he was a genius; but he wasn't born one. He was, according to his biography, an ordinary boy. He just worked hard, tried and tried again. He never stopped being curious, never shied away from taking on a new challenge.

Charles Darwin is often called a genius, too. And they can be little doubt that his seminal book, 'The Origin of Species', has been life-changing and paradigm-shifting. But it was the result of years of research, a lot of effort and toil, and a lot of team-work involving hundreds of discussions with colleagues and mentors. The book went through several drafts and took Darwin half a lifetime to finalise. His book wasn't created in a big bang, it slowly evolved over time.

The musical 'genius' Mozart wrote and performed music for over ten years before producing anything that we would deem a masterpiece today. Before his effort and practice had paid off, he produced work which was considered ordinary and unoriginal.

CHAPTER SEVEN

Some of us are more equal than others

So are we all created equal? Is the concept of gifted and talented a myth? Well, no, not quite. It seems there are some children who are born with a special aptitude or 'gift' but it is their love of learning and challenge, their hard work and purposeful practice that really sets them apart. In other words, their 'gift' is not, as most people believe, their innate ability; it is the drive or intrinsic motivation they possess that feeds their endless curiosity and their pursuit of challenge. Darwin's gift was not his scientific ability but the fact he collected specimens non-stop from early childhood. Mozart's gift was not his musical ability but the fact he worked so hard to improve his performance that his hands became deformed. As Dweck says, "We all have interests that can blossom into abilities". Yes, it is true that some people simply acquire skills naturally and with very little effort whereas others have to work hard at it. But just because some people can do something with little effort or training, it doesn't mean that others can't do it - and often even better - with training.

This makes me wonder how much 'talent' is being wasted in our schools through lack of effort or through lack of awareness. How many students are not being encouraged to try harder, are being told that they do not have the ability to succeed in a certain subject and so simply do not try? How many teachers underestimate students' potential to develop and improve? In her book 'Mindset', Carol Dweck recounts the story of an American teacher working in one of the worst schools in Los Angeles. The students were, to put it mildly, apathetic. But their teacher, applying a growth mindset, asked himself 'How can I teach them?' instead of 'Can I teach them?', and 'How will they learn best?' rather than 'Can they learn?' Instead of doing what many schools still do with those students who fall behind - give them scaffolded ('easier') materials or put them in for a different tier ('easier') exam paper - he decided to challenge them, to stretch them. He taught them university-level calculus and took them to the top of the national charts in Maths.

The idea that students who fall behind need 'dumbed down' work, simplified work drummed into them over and over again, is certainly a fixed mindset approach for it assumes these students cannot handle more. But the results are nearly always depressing: students do not learn anything new and therefore make little or no progress.

CHAPTER EIGHT

Lowering standards does not raise attainment

Many teachers still think, as the colleague I mentioned earlier did, that lowering standards will give students the experience of success, boost their self-esteem, and raise their achievement. But all the evidence suggests it doesn't work. Instead, it just leads to poorly educated children. These teachers do not teach, they judge. They look at students' opening performance and decide who's smart and who's not. Then they give up on the 'thick' ones.

Great teachers, by contrast, believe in the growth of the intellect and talent, and they are fascinated by the process of learning. Great teachers set high standards for all their students, not just the ones who are already achieving. They create an atmosphere of trust, not judgment. They say 'I am going to teach you' not 'I am going to judge you.'

In other words, and to return to my opening line: great teachers are teachers not judges.

The educational researcher, Benjamin Bloom, studied one hundred and twenty outstanding achievers. They were concert pianists, artists, Olympic swimmers, world-class tennis players, mathematicians and neurologists. Most of them were not that remarkable as children and didn't show clear talent before they began their formal training. Even by early adolescence, it was impossible to predict their future accomplishments by dent of their current ability. Only their continued motivation and commitment, along with their network of support, took them to the top. Bloom concluded that, "After forty years of intensive research on school learning in the United States as well as abroad, my major conclusion is: what any person in the world can learn, almost all persons can learn, if provided with the appropriate prior and current conditions of learning".

I believe that Bloom's research calls into question the very notion of setting or banding students by ability. We commonly use test scores and teacher assessments to sort students into groups of similar ability...but test scores and teacher assessments only tell us where a student is now not where a student could end up.

Falko Rheinberg, a researcher in Germany, studied schoolteachers with different mindsets. Some of the teachers had fixed mindsets and believed that students entering a class with different achievement levels were deeply and permanently different. These students started and ended the year in the top set or the bottom set. But some teachers had a growth mindset and believed that all students could develop their skills. In their classrooms it didn't matter whether students started the year in a top or bottom set, both groups ended the year with performances befitting a top set. The difference between the sets simply disappeared under the teachers who taught for improvement because these teachers found a way to reach the 'low ability' students.

CHAPTER NINE

What is the secret of success?

Human beings have a biological drive that includes hunger, thirst and sex. We also have another long-recognised drive: the drive that responds to rewards and punishments. But scientists are now discovering that humans have a third drive, what some call 'intrinsic motivation'. This third drive is the subject of a book by the American writer Daniel H. Pink. In 'Drive', he argues that rewards don't work. Instead, they "encourage unethical behaviour, create addictions, and foster short-term thinking". It's hard to disagree in this current economic climate. We are living in a period of austerity brought about by so-called 'casino banking' and yet, whilst most of us tighten our belts to weather the economic storm (to mix metaphors), bankers are rewarding themselves multi-million pound bonuses. Barclays boss, Bob Diamond, was in the news in July 2012 because his bank stood accused of manipulating LIBOR rates - the rate at which it borrows money - in order to keep its rates of lending to customers artificially high. Diamond lost his job but stood to receive millions in severance pay. It seems big pay rewards in the city have led to unethical behaviour in which bankers profit from customer's hardship, and to short-term thinking in which boom inevitably leads to bust.

Pink calls this type of behaviour - the drive that responds to rewards and punishments - Type X behaviour. He says Type X behaviour is "fuelled more by extrinsic desires than intrinsic ones and concerned less with the inherent satisfaction of an activity and more with the external rewards to which an activity leads"

It's time for a change. Not only does Type X behaviour lead to unethical acts, it also has a short shelf-life. People do not remain motivated for long. They lose interest in the thing they're doing. They are only interested in the rewards that the task brings. And their performance suffers. They stop getting better at it. They stop learning.

Professor Guy Claxton says that "one of the most reliable sources of happiness [is] learning. People report feeling happy when they are engaged in wrestling with something difficult but worthwhile; when they feel in charge, and are not criticised by others." He comes to the important conclusion that "if we want our children to be happy we need to help them to discover the 'joy of struggle' and understand and develop the craft of worthwhile learning". In other words, we need to teach our students the importance of intrinsic motivation, of enjoying learning for learning's sake not because it leads to extrinsic rewards. In some senses, this means we must stop 'teaching to the test' - students must perceive the end result of their learning, not as a certificate, but as the acquisition of new knowledge, experiences and skills.

In 'Drive' Daniel Pink recounts the experiments conducted by Harry Harlow and Edward Deci. Harlow was a professor of psychology at the University of Wisconsin and studied primate behaviour in the 1940s. In 1949 Harlow and two colleagues carried out a two-week experiment on eight rhesus monkeys. They devised a simple mechanical puzzle which could be solved by pulling out a vertical pin, undoing a hook and lifting a hinged door. The researchers placed the puzzles in the monkeys' cages to observe how they reacted. Almost immediately, without any prompting, the monkeys began playing with the puzzles with what Harlow described as focus, determination and enjoyment.

Relatively quickly the monkeys began figuring the mechanism out. By days 13 and 14 the monkeys had become adept: they could solve the puzzles quickly; indeed, two-thirds of them did so in less than a minute. Nobody had taught the monkeys how to do it and they had received no reward for doing so. This behaviour was contrary to what we know of primates. As I have said, there are two drives that power our behaviour: a biological drive such as the need for food, water and copulation in order to satiate hunger, quench thirst and satisfy carnal needs - in other words, the internal drive; and the external drive in which we behave in certain ways in order to be rewarded or in order to avoid punishments. If people knew they would to be paid for doing something, or they would be fined for not doing it, they would be more motivated to do it.

However, in this experiment the "solution did not lead to food, water or sex gratification" as Harlow explained. Nor did it lead to rewards, not even affection or a round of applause. Harlow was perplexed. He wrote, "The behaviour obtained in this investigation poses some interesting questions for motivation theory, since significant learning was attained and efficient performance maintained without resort to special or extrinsic incentives".

To try explain this anomaly, Harlow offered a new theory: he proposed a third drive. "The performance of the task provided intrinsic reward." In other words, the monkeys solved the puzzles and got better and quicker at solving them simply because they enjoyed doing so, they found it gratifying.   The task was its own reward. Harlow eventually called this 'intrinsic motivation'.

Harlow wanted to know whether their performance would improve further if rewards were introduced. When he tested the theory, he found something astonishing: the monkeys actually made more errors and solved the puzzles slower and less frequently when rewards were at stake. "The introduction of food in the present experiment served to disrupt performance," he said.

Harlow concluded that this third drive, or intrinsic motivation, "may be as basic and strong as the [biological drive and the drive powered by rewards and punishments].   Furthermore, there is some reason to believe that [the third drive] can be as efficient in facilitating learning."

Twenty years later, in 1969, a Carnegie Mellon University psychology graduate, Edward Deci, studied the notion of intrinsic motivation for his dissertation using a group of male and female university students. He choose a Soma puzzle cube which consisted of seven plastic pieces, six with four one-inch cubes and one with three one-inch cubes. The pieces could be arranged into several million combinations.   Deci divided his participants into Group A - an experimental group, and Group B - a control group. Each group took part in three hour-long sessions on consecutive days.   Each participant was given seven Soma puzzle pieces, illustrations depicting three puzzle combinations and a copy of Time magazine, The New Yorker and Playboy. Deci explained the instructions and timed the students using a stopwatch.

In the first session, participants in Groups A and B had to assemble their pieces into the combinations shown in the illustrations. In the second session, they did the same thing with different illustrations but this time Deci told Group A they'd be paid $1 for every one they got right. Group B were not paid. In the third session, both groups received new illustrations and neither group was paid.

Halfway through each session, Deci stopped the participants after they had assembled two of the three combinations and gave them a fourth drawing. In order to choose the right combination, he said, he had to feed the results into a computer which would take several minutes. Deci left the room ostensibly to use the computer but actually observed the participants from behind a two-way mirror. He told them as he was leaving, "I shall be gone only a few minutes, you may do whatever you like while I'm gone". He watched them for exactly eight minutes.

In the first session there was little difference between Group A and Group B: both sets of participants continued playing with the puzzles for about three to four minutes. After which time, presumably, they would flick through the magazines or sit idle. In the second session, when Group A was being paid to complete the puzzles and Group B was not, Group B continued to behave as they had the previous day - they played with the puzzles for about half their free time. But Group A spent more time playing with the puzzles, about five minutes on average. So far so predictable. When being paid, the participants wanted to get a head-start so that they earned more money. This proved the second drive: reward someone and they will be motivated to work harder.

In the third session, however, something strange happened. Group A and B were now unpaid - Group A were told there wasn't enough money to pay them for a second day. When left alone for eight minutes, Group B played with the puzzles for a little longer than they had previously, suggesting that, over time, they were becoming more engaged in the task. But Group A now spent significantly less time playing with the puzzles, on average two minutes less than they had previously when being paid, suggesting they now enjoyed the task less.

This experiment echoed what Harlow had discovered twenty years earlier: "When money is used as an external reward for some activity, the subjects lose intrinsic interest for the activity," wrote Deci. Rewards encouraged short-term increases in productivity but the effect wore off and eventually reduced the person's motivation for the task. Deci concluded that we have an "inherent tendency to seek out novelty and challenges, to extend and exercise [our] capacities, to explore, and to learn".

But Deci echoed Alfred Binet when he said that intrinsic motivation required the right environment - what Binet had called 'method'. Deci said, "One who is interested in developing and enhancing intrinsic motivation in children, employees, students, etc., should not concentrate on external-control systems such as monetary reward".

Rewards, it seems, have a negative effect.

CHAPTER TEN

Just for the fun of it

Returning to 'Drive', Daniel Pink says that Type I behaviour (unlike Type X which - as I have already said - is "fuelled more by extrinsic desires than intrinsic ones and concerned less with the inherent satisfaction of an activity and more with the external rewards to which an activity leads") is concerned "more with the inherent satisfaction of the activity itself". This third drive, or intrinsic motivation, is - according to Pink - three-fold:

1. Autonomy - the desire to direct our own lives
2. Mastery - the urge to get better and better at something that matters
3. Purpose - the yearning to do what we do in the service of something larger than ourselves

Let's look at what each of these aspects of intrinsic motivation means...

Autonomy: Pink says that "people need autonomy over task (what they do), time (when they do it), team (who they do it with), and technique (how they do it)". The theory being this: if someone is in control of their activities, they are more likely to be motivated by them and more likely to excel at them.

Mastery: Pink says that "only engagement can produce mastery - becoming better at something that matters". He goes on to say that "mastery begins with 'flow' - optimal experiences when the challenges we face are exquisitely matched to our abilities - [and] requires the capacity to see your abilities not as finite, but as infinitely improvable." Again, this is about the desire to improve, to want to get better and better at something. People are only motivated to get better at something they are engaged in and enjoy. Pink goes on to say that "Mastery is a pain: it demands effort, grit and deliberate practice. And mastery is asymptote: it's impossible to fully realise, which makes it simultaneously frustrating and alluring."

Purpose: Humans seek purpose, "a cause greater and more enduring than themselves". This is to say that people need to feel that what they are doing will have a long-term purpose and meaning in the world. It's the desire to leave your mark on the world, to do something worthwhile and with impact.

Pink provides a useful example of the power of autonomy, mastery and purpose in action. He takes us back to 1995 and asks an economist to consider two business models, each concerned with developing a new encyclopaedia: the first model comes from Microsoft, a multi-million pound global organisation; the other is the result of a not-for-profit 'hobby'. Microsoft's encyclopaedia involves a band of paid professional writers and editors working for well-paid managers who oversee a project which is delivered on time and on budget. Microsoft sell the encyclopaedia on CD-ROMs and online. The hobbyists, meanwhile, do not belong to a company and are not paid. Instead, tens of thousands of people write and edit entries in the encyclopaedia just for fun. Contributors offer their time and expertise for nothing and the encyclopaedia itself is offered free of charge to anyone who wants it via the internet. Clearly, any economist worth his or her salt would predict that the first business model led by Microsoft would go on to thrive whilst the second model would falter. But by 2009, Microsoft had discontinued 'Encarta' whilst 'Wikipedia' continued to thrive - with 13 million entries in 260 languages, it had become the largest and most popular encyclopaedia in the world. The business model that relied on traditional rewards to motivate its employees and customers had failed; the one that relied on intrinsic motivation (doing something simply for the fun of it) had succeeded; in the battle for supremacy, money had lost to the love of learning.

CHAPTER ELEVEN

A license to kill...with praise

To take Pink's notion of Type X behaviour further, let us consider just how damaging praise can be. Pink says that being motivated by extrinsic desires leads, at best, to short-termism whereby someone loses interest in what they are doing because they are doing it, not for the enjoyment and interest in the thing itself, but for other rewards.

Dr Carol S. Dweck goes further in her cautionary assessment of the dangers of rewards. She conducted research with hundreds of students, mostly early adolescents. She gave each student a set of ten fairly different problems to solve from a non-verbal IQ test. Most of the students did pretty well and when they'd finished, she praised them. She praised some of the students for their ability (eg, 'You got such a high score, you must be really smart'); she praised the others for their effort (eg, 'You got such a high score, you must have worked really hard'). Both groups were exactly equal to begin with. But after receiving praise, they began to differ. The students whose ability was praised were pushed into the fixed mindset. When they were given a choice, they rejected a challenging new task that they could learn from, favouring more of the same instead. Why? Because they didn't want to do anything which would expose flaws in their intelligence and bring their talent into question. In contrast, 90% of the students whose effort was praised wanted to try the challenging new task precisely because they could learn from it.

All the students were given new challenging tasks to do. None of the students did particularly well. Those who were praised for their ability now thought they weren't very smart after all because, if success means they are intelligent, then failure must mean they're deficient. Those praised for effort, on the other hand, didn't see it as failure. They believed it meant they had to try harder. As for the students' enjoyment of the task, all students enjoyed the first task but those praised for ability did not enjoy the harder task because it isn't fun when your talent is called into question. Those praised for effort, however, said they still enjoyed it and indeed some felt the harder task was more fun because they had to exert more effort in order to try complete it.

As the tests were IQ tests, Dweck concluded that praising ability actually lowered students' IQs whereas praising effort raised them. Dweck also states that praising children's intelligence harms their motivation and harms their performance. Why? Because although children love to be praised, especially for their talents, as soon as they hit a snag their confidence goes out of the window and their motivation hits rock bottom. If success means they're smart, then failure means they're dumb.

Dweck talks about hidden messages in the praise we give our children. The statement, 'You learned that so quickly, you must be really smart' can be translated in a child's mind to: 'If I don't learn something quickly, I'm not smart'. Similarly, the statement 'You're so brilliant, you got an A without even trying' can be translated in a child's mind to: 'I'd better quit whilst I'm ahead or they won't think I'm smart anymore'.

This doesn't mean we shouldn't praise children, Dweck argues. But it does mean we should only use a certain type of praise. We can praise our students as much as we want for the "growth-oriented process - what they accomplished through practice, study, persistence, and good strategies". But we should avoid the kind of praise that judges their intelligence or talent, and we should avoid the kind of praise that implies "we're proud of them for their intelligence or talent rather than for the work they put in".

CHAPTER TWELVE

Practice makes perfect

So far Alfred Binet and Carol Dweck have argued the importance of practice, training and method over innate ability or intelligence. Dweck has also said we should avoid praising intelligence because it is counter-productive. Daniel Pink has asserted that rewards can lead to unethical behaviour and short-term thinking, whereas intrinsic motivation - doing something because you enjoy it and want to get better at it - is a positive driving force for good and leads to long-term learning. Now let's look in more detail at what constitutes good practice, training and method. Let's consider why effort is more important than talent, why Type I behaviour is more effective than Type X...

Matthew Syed is three-time Commonwealth table-tennis champion. In 1995 at the tender age of 25, he became the British number one. To put that into some kind of perspective, there are 2.4 million players in Britain, 30,000 paid up members of the governing body and thousands of teams. So what marked Syed out for excellence? Was it his speed, guile, mental strength, agility and reflexes? There was certainly no silver spoon, no nepotism. He came from an ordinary family in an ordinary suburb of an ordinary town in south-east England.

In his book, 'Bounce', Syed argues that "we like to think that sport is a meritocracy - where achievement is driven by ability and hard work - but it is nothing of the sort". He goes on to say that, "Practically every man and woman who triumphs against the odds is, on closer inspection, a beneficiary of unusual circumstances. The delusion lies in focusing on the individuality of their triumph without perceiving - or bothering to look for - the powerful opportunities stacked in their favour."

Syed says his was not a triumph of individuality, a personal odyssey of success, or a triumph against the odds; it was the result of a fortunate set of circumstances. His parents bought him a table-tennis table and they were lucky enough to have a garage big enough to house it. He had a brother who loved table-tennis as much as he did and with whom he could practice daily. He had a teacher who just happened to be the nation's top coach and a senior figure in the Table Tennis Association. His local club, Omega, was open 24 hours a day and gave out keys to its select group of members so that they could practice endlessly at any time of day and night.

As a result of these circumstances, the local area produced a number of top players not just Syed. His brother won three national titles; one of the top female players of her generation lived in the house opposite and won countless junior titles and a national senior title; in-between their two houses lived another successful player who went on to win a series of doubles titles. There were other outstanding players in the neighbourhood, too, which meant that this one ordinary street in Reading produced more outstanding table tennis players than the rest of the country put together.

This supports Malcolm Gladwell's argument (in his book, 'Outliers') that outstanding performance is not about 'who you are' but rather 'what you do' and 'where you come from'.

CHAPTER THIRTEEN

The talent iceberg

So what is talent? Anders Ericsson, a psychologist at Florida State University, conducted an investigation into the causes of outstanding performance. His subjects were violinists from the Music Academy of West Berlin. He divided his subjects into three groups: the first group were the outstanding violinists who were expected to become soloists; the second group were very good (though not as accomplished as the first group) and were expected to join the world's top orchestras; the third group were good but the least able and were expected to become music teachers (no offence to the music teachers reading this). The 'setting' of the three groups was based on assessment conducted by the academy's professors and on the level of success the students had enjoyed in open competitions.

The biographical details of all the students were very similar with no systematic differences: they each began playing the violin when they were aged 8; they each decided to become musicians when they were 14; they each had the same number of music teachers and had studied the same number of musical instruments beyond the violin. In fact, there was only one difference but it was quite a striking one: the number of hours they had devoted to practice.

By the age of twenty, the students in the first group had practised an average of ten thousand hours which is over two thousand hours more than the second group and over six thousand hours more than the third group. Ericsson found that there were no exceptions to this pattern: nobody in the first group who had reached the top of their game had done so without copious amounts of practice; and nobody who had worked so hard had failed to excel. The only distinguishing feature between the best and the rest was purposeful practice.

Jack Nicklaus, the most successful golfer of all time, has said the same thing: "Nobody - but nobody - has ever become really proficient at golf without practice, without doing a lot of thinking and then hitting a lot of shots. It isn't so much a lack of talent; it's a lack of being able to repeat good shots consistently that frustrates most players. And the only answer to that is practice."

Syed quantifies the amount of 'purposeful practice' that is required to achieve excellence. He points out that extensive research has come up with a specific answer: "from art to science and from board games to tennis, it has been found that a minimum of ten years is required to reach world-class status in any complex task". Malcolm Gladwell, meanwhile, asserts that most top performers practise for around one thousand hours per year.

There is a logic here: if someone believes that attaining excellence relies solely on talent, they are more likely to give up if they do not show early promise. However, if they believe that talent is not a (or is not the only) factor in achieving excellence then they are more likely to persevere.

Anders Ericsson calls talent the 'iceberg illusion'. In other words, when we witness excellence we are witnessing the end product of a process that took years to realise. The countless hours of practice that have gone into this end result of excellence are invisible to us - they are submerged beneath the icy waters leaving only the tip of excellence visible.

Syed says that "world class performance comes by striving for a target just out of reach, but with a vivid awareness of how the gap might be breached". This is why great teachers do not 'dumb down' but provide real challenge for their students

Syed says that "ten thousand hours of purposeful practice" is required to achieve excellence. By 'purposeful' he means "concentration and dedication" but also having "access to the right training system, and that sometimes means living in the right town or having the right coach". This is a version of what Binet called "practice, training, and method". When we transfer the idea of excellence to schools, having the right training system or method is easier to realise and less concerned with good fortune. It is about teachers creating the right conditions in their classrooms for learning to take place. It is about providing challenge, not 'dumbing down'; it is about providing a safe and secure atmosphere in which it is not only acceptable to make mistakes but it is positively encouraged because to make mistakes is to learn.

Syed cites the Olympic figure-skater Shizuka Arakawa as an example of the importance of making mistakes. Arakawa fell down more than twenty thousand times in her pursuit of excellence. Syed says, "When examining [Shizuka's] story, the one question...to ask was: Why would anyone endure all that? Why would she keep striving in the teeth of constant failure? Why not give up and try something else?... It is because she did not interpret falling down as failure. Armed with a growth mindset, she interpreted falling down not merely as a means of improving, but as evidence that she was improving. Failure was not something that sapped her energy and vitality, but something that provided her with an opportunity to learn, develop, and adapt." In this sense, Arakawa is like my youngest daughter, falling down is evidence she is getting better at walking.

If this seems odd, Syed reminds us that in an advert for Nike, Michael Jordan declared: "I've missed more than nine thousand shots. I've lost almost three hundred games. Twenty-six times I've been trusted to take the game-winning shot and missed." In other words, in order to become the greatest basketball player of all time, Jordan had first to embrace failure. Jordan has said that "mental toughness and heart are a lot stronger than some of the physical advantages you might have." Thomas Edison, who I have already mentioned, said the same thing: "If I find 10,000 ways something won't work, I haven't failed. I am not discouraged, because every wrong attempt discarded is another step forward."

In 'Bounce', Syed asks us to think of life having two paths: one leading to mediocrity, the other to excellence. The path to mediocrity, he says, is "flat and straight [and] it is possible to cruise along on autopilot with a nice, smooth, steady, almost effortless progression [and] you can reach your destination without stumbling and falling over". The path to excellence, meanwhile, "could not be more different...it is steep, gruelling, and arduous. It is inordinately lengthy, requiring a minimum of ten thousand hours of lung-busting effort to get to the summit [and] it forces voyagers to stumble and fall on every single stretch of the journey." Excellence, after all, is about "striving for what is just out of reach and not quite making it; it is about grappling with tasks beyond current limitations and falling short again and again."

CHAPTER FOURTEEN

A tour de force at the Tour de France

Here's one final - and, at the time of writing, contemporary - example to exemplify what Syed and others have said...

Cyclist Bradley Wiggins took the path to excellence in 2012 and won the Tour de France in what Sir Chris Hoy described as "the greatest sporting achievement by any British athlete ever". And yet few of those who met Wiggins during his formative years thought he was a potential Tour winner. Wiggins's first coach, Sean Bannister, told The Guardian: "I didn't think for a second he would be a Grand Tour contender, but no one knows at that stage in a rider's development."

So his journey towards the ultimate prize in cycling was not pre-ordained: he was not a natural born genius; he did not possess innate athletic prowess. But he did work hard. He enjoyed some success as a youngster but his record speaks for itself: he got better and better with age and experience.

His manager John Herety said Wiggins worked hard and did his research: "He had a wealth of knowledge of road racing. He knew all about the riders with a fan's passion as opposed to someone who is definitely headed in that direction". Matt Parker, who trained Wiggins for the 2008 Beijing Olympics, said that the key to Wiggins's success was his commitment: "Not many would sign up [for that amount of hard work]," he said. Fellow British rider, David Millar, says Wiggins is "dedicated, driven, self-obsessed and ultimately sensible".

Wiggins had to wait until his early 30s to achieve these heady heights. Although he won a range of titles including his first junior title in 1998, he didn't fulfil his potential early in his career and even his Olympic medals were the result of reserved - dare I say, second-rate - performances. Shane Sutton, his current coach, believes this is because he "never really trained [hard enough]. He didn't really apply himself as well as he could".

The secret of his Tour de France success in 2012, therefore, can be put down to practice, training, and above all, method...

Practice: Wiggins adopted a no-compromise approach: he devoted himself to practising 365 days a year rather than resting in late autumn as he had previously. His coach, Sutton, said Wiggins was "willing to give it 100%" this time.

Training: Wiggins began training earlier in the year than is usual and, rather than a gradual build-up, he rode at intensities which he would not normally reach until well into the racing season. Wiggins said: "[We] took the swimming approach where [we] train the top end constantly throughout the year... [we have] totally revolutionised the way we train." This revolutionary training schedule meant he was able to deal with more demanding workloads and pressures.

Method: His Tour win was masterminded by his coaches Tim Kerrison and Shane Sutton. They broke down each element required to win and were responsible for Wiggins's day-to-day training. They radically changed Wiggins's training schedule and introduced a lot of high-altitude warm-weather training sessions. Wiggins also raced less often but always raced to win. This took the pressure off him because he went into the Tour with a perfect record behind him. It also meant that he was more at ease with leading a race rather than chasing one.

So Wiggins's success can be attributed, not to innate intellect or ability, but to practice, training, and above all, method.

CHAPTER FIFTEEN

IQ versus EQ

So far, we have challenged IQ as a measure of innate ability and intellect and argued instead that hard work and practice are more important than natural aptitude when it comes to achieving one's true potential. We have also considered the importance of intrinsic motivation - the desire to complete tasks for the intrinsic enjoyment of them rather than for extrinsic rewards. And we have considered the importance of having a 'growth mindset' - as opposed to a 'fixed mindset' - of believing that you can cultivate important qualities through effort; of believing that - although people's initial talents and aptitudes, interests, or temperaments may differ - everyone can change and grow through application and experience.

In short, we have said that a person's true potential is unknown (and unknowable) and that it is impossible to foresee what can be accomplished with years of, what Dweck calls, "passion, toil, and training".

Now let us look at an alternative to IQ: EQ, or emotional intelligence. EQ is concerned with a person's emotional awareness and social skills; it centres on the belief that anyone can develop his or her emotional intelligence in order to become more successful. After all, if you develop your sense of self-awareness and self-management, then you improve your confidence, tolerance and chances of success. People with a growth mindset are emotionally intelligent because they are aware of their strengths and weaknesses and are eager to overcome those weaknesses through learning and hard work. Emotionally intelligent people are resilient - they see making mistakes as a challenge not as a failure. Emotionally intelligent people are optimistic and empathetic towards others. In this sense, EQ is more important than IQ because, as Daniel Goleman says, "emotional intelligence is a master aptitude that profoundly affects all other abilities".

EQ is important to teachers, too, because developing students' emotional competencies and social skills are a means of raising attainment and, more importantly, of preparing students for life after school.

Emotional intelligence is often cited as an antidote to IQ: it is about the ability to identify, assess, and control your own and others' emotions. It is primarily concerned with non-cognitive skills - in other words, those concerned with personality and social skills, not intellect or ability. In this sense, it supports our hypothesis that IQ, as we know it, is a myth because everyone can develop his or her emotional and social skills in order to grow his or her intelligence.

Although Daniel Goleman is often credited with bringing emotional intelligence into popular culture with his 1995 book of the same name, its history can be traced back as far as Charles Darwin who studied the importance of emotional expression on a species's survival and on its ability to adapt to its ever-evolving environment.

In the 1900s, even though traditional definitions of intelligence emphasised cognitive ability such as memory and problem-solving, a number of researchers began to recognise the importance of non-cognitive elements such as understanding and responding to other people's feelings. In 1920, E.L. Thorndike coined the term 'social intelligence' to describe the skill of understanding and managing other people. In 1940, David Wechsler described the influence of non-intellective factors on intelligent behaviour. Wechsler argued that traditional models of intelligence could not be complete until we could adequately describe these non-intellective factors.

More recently, Howard Gardner has asserted that traditional types of intelligence, such as IQ, fail to explain cognitive ability. In 1983, Gardner's book 'Frames of Mind: The Theory of Multiple Intelligences' introduced the idea of multiple intelligences which includes inter-personal intelligence (the capacity to understand the intentions, motivations and desires of other people) and intra-personal intelligence (the capacity to understand yourself and appreciate your own feelings, fears and motivations).

CHAPTER SIXTEEN

Ability EQ and Trait EQ

Since 2000, there have emerged two main models of Emotional Intelligence: Ability EQ and Trait EQ.

Ability EQ, as defined by Salovery and Mayer, is the belief that emotions are sources of information that help people to make sense of their social environment. Salovery and Mayer propose that individuals' abilities to process emotional information differs greatly, as do their abilities to relate their emotional processing to a wider cognition. According to Salovery and Mayer's book, 'What is Emotional Intelligence?'', there are four types of Ability EQ:

1. Perceiving emotions – the ability to detect and decipher emotions in faces, pictures, voices, and cultural artefacts—including the ability to identify your own emotions. Recognising and understanding emotions represents a basic aspect of emotional intelligence because it makes possible all other processing of emotional information.

2. Using emotions – the ability to harness emotions in order to facilitate various cognitive activities, such as thinking and problem solving. An emotionally intelligent person can capitalise on his or her changing moods in order to match the task in hand.

3. Understanding emotions – the ability to process and understand emotional language, and the ability to appreciate complicated emotional relationships. The ability to understand emotions encompasses the ability to be sensitive to slight variations in emotions, and the ability to recognise and describe how emotions change over time.

4. Managing emotions – the ability to regulate emotions in ourselves and others. Therefore, the emotionally intelligent person can harness emotions, even negative ones, and manage them in order to achieve his or her goals.

Trait EQ - the second model - by contrast, refers to someone's perception of their own emotional abilities. This definition of EQ encompasses behavioural tendencies and abilities and is measured by self-report, as opposed to the ability-based model which refers to actual abilities that have proven highly resistant to scientific measurement.

According to the psychologist Konstantin Vasily Petrides, "the conceptualisation of EQ as a personality trait leads to a construct that lies outside the taxonomy of human cognitive ability". As such, none of the measures of Trait EQ assess intelligence, ability, or skill. Instead - if we use the most comprehensive measure, the 'Trait Emotional Intelligence Questionnaire', as our guide - they measure such traits as well-being, self-control, emotionality, and sociability.

Daniel Goleman further developed the Trait EQ model in his book 'Emotional Intelligence: Why it can matter more than IQ'. Goleman focused on EQ as a range of competencies and skills which can drive performance. Goleman's model outlined five main aspects of emotional intelligence:

1. Self-awareness – the ability to recognise your own emotions, strengths, weaknesses, drives, values and goals, and to recognise their impact on others.

2. Self-regulation – this is about controlling your disruptive emotions and impulses, and adapting to changing circumstances.

3. Social skill – this is about managing relationships in order to move people in the right direction.

4. Empathy - this is about considering other people's feelings especially when making decisions.

5. Motivation - this is about being driven to achieve success for the sake of achievement.

Goleman's book also proposed a set of emotional competencies. These competencies, Goleman argued, are not innate talents, but rather learned capabilities that must be worked on and can be developed in order to achieve outstanding performance. And this is the crux of the matter: emotional intelligence encompasses personality and social skills which can be learned and developed over time in order to achieve greater levels of success. In this sense, Goleman builds on what we have already explored: although he believes that individuals are born with a general emotional intelligence, he argues that everyone has the potential to improve their emotional competencies. Learning and developing emotional and social skills helps everyone to improve their performance and get better results.

CHAPTER SEVENTEEN

EQ in schools

Schools in the United States recognised the importance of EQ in the late 1970s with the introduction of the self-science curriculum and schools in the UK began to recognise its importance in the mid-2000s with the introduction of SEAL (social and emotional aspects of learning) and PLTS (personal, learning and thinking skills), both underpinned by the new national curriculum in England and Wales which had as its central tenet the following key aim: to develop successful learners, confident individuals, and responsible citizens. Learning to Learn - which includes the use of Gardner's multiple intelligences and Guy Claxton's 4Rs - among other constructs - has also become commonplace in English schools in recent years.

There are many interpretations of just what form these 'social and emotional aspects of learning' should take in practice and of what students should be taught in schools. In 1978, the Self-Science Curriculum in the US, which was developed by Karen Stone and Harold Dillehunt, decided the following skills were important:

self-awareness; personal decision-making; managing feelings; handling stress; empathy; communications; self-disclosure; insight; self-acceptance; personal responsibility; assertiveness; group dynamics; and conflict resolution.

Slightly later, the W T Grant Consortium's 'Active Ingredients of Prevention Programs', which was primarily a drug and alcohol prevention curriculum in schools and was aimed at developing social competences, choose to have the following key ingredients:

Emotional skills: identifying and labelling feelings; expressing feelings; assessing the intensity of feelings; managing feelings; delaying gratification; controlling impulses; reducing stress; knowing the difference between feelings and actions.

Cognitive skills: self-talk - conducting an 'inner dialogue' as a way to cope with a topic or challenge or reinforce one's own behaviour; reading and interpreting social cues - for example, recognising social influences on behaviour and seeing oneself in the perspective of the larger community; using steps for problem-solving and decision-making - for instance, controlling impulses, setting goals, identifying alternative actions, anticipating consequences; understanding the perspective of others; understanding behavioural norms; a positive attitude towards life; self-awareness - for example, developing realistic expectations about oneself.

Behavioural skills: non-verbal - communicating through eye contact, facial expressiveness, tone of voice, gestures and so on; verbal - making clear requests, responding effectively to criticism, resisting negative influences, listening to others, helping others, participating in positive peer groups.

In the UK, the government-led SEAL initiative was built around these (somewhat familiar) elements:

1. Self-awareness - knowing and valuing myself and understanding how I think and feel.

2. Managing feelings - managing how we express emotions, coping with and changing difficult and uncomfortable feelings, and increasing and enhancing positive and pleasant feelings.

3. Motivation - working towards goals, and being more persistent, resilient and optimistic.

4. Empathy - understanding others' thoughts and feelings and valuing and supporting others.

5. Social skills - building and maintaining relationships and solving problems.

These five SEAL - which have lost some of their importance since a change of government in 2010 - are intended to help students to: learn to manage their impulses, helping them settle quickly, concentrate and not disrupt others; build warm relationships, which help them to care what others (e.g. staff and peers) think and to respond positively to them; manage strong and uncomfortable emotions such as anger and frustration, and become more resilient, which helps them rise to the challenges of the learning process and stick at it if things get tough; learn to feel good about themselves, which reduces the likelihood of disruptive behaviour and increases capacity for independent learning; manage anxiety and stress, including around tests and examinations; learn to empathise, for example with other students' desire to learn, which helps them contribute to a positive learning environment; reflect on longer term goals, which helps them see the point of learning, raise their aspirations and become more able to resist negative pressure from others; feel optimistic about themselves and their ability to learn, which improves their motivation to work hard and attend regularly.

Alongside SEAL, and an intrinsic part of the national curriculum, are six Personal Learning and Thinking Skills (PLTS): independent enquirers; creative thinkers; team workers; self-managers; effective participators; reflective learners.

These PLTS are intended to underpin the whole curriculum and they aim to encourage students' engagement with their learning. For example, the PLTS increase learners' understanding of themselves as well as their relationship with others and the world around them. It is expected that effective teaching of PLTS will help students to raise achievement and will make a considerable impact on students' abilities to succeed, both now and in later life.

CHAPTER EIGHTEEN

Why do we need EQ?

Whatever acronym is given to it, it is clear that schools are beginning to recognise the importance of teaching social and emotional skills to their students as a means of preparing them for life and, more central to the subject of this book, as a means of helping young people to grow their own intelligence.

Teaching emotional intelligence is also necessary because the world is changing: economically, socially and culturally.

The world is changing economically. Schools are often seen as an investment in the country's competitiveness in world markets and as an investment in its future prosperity: schools are tasked with producing a future workforce which is highly skilled, creative and adaptable, a workforce which can compete in global markets. In order to do this, schools need to produce young people with social skills and emotional competencies. Schools need to keep up with 21st Century employers. Their curricula need to cultivate transferrable skills and attitudes; they need to prepare children for an uncertain world of increasing pressures.

The world is changing socially. Young people are finding growing up in the 21st Century increasingly difficult. They are exposed to growing pressures and uncertainties about their sense of identity, their sexuality, their friendships, relationships and loyalty, and about their safety. As Professor Guy Claxton says, "Whether young people flounder or flourish in the wider maelstrom of conflicting images and ideas depends on the resources they have at their disposal. To swim or sink demands a high level of mental and emotional development."

Although the UK's coalition government favour a return to 1950s-style schooling in which students recite poetry and learn by rote the kings and queens of England, a more significant body of opinion believes it is now the job of education to help young people develop resilience and resourcefulness, and the transferrable skills and abilities needed to deal with the world, not simply operate a 'knowledge dump'.

The world is changing culturally, too. Technology is now at the heart of what we do and how we live. We are no longer training young people to work on production lines - after all, why teach students to do things that machines and computers can do? Equally, why teach something they could learn from machines and computers?

Of course, there are implications of teaching emotional intelligence in schools for our education system, not least on our processes of assessment. At the moment success or failure in school is judged by how many GCSEs and A Levels a student gets at grade C and above; it is not judged by how emotionally intelligent they have become, by how motivated they are, how empathetic they are towards others, how good they are at team-working and how accurate their self-awareness is. If schools are to teach emotional intelligence then there has to be another measure of success in school which is widely recognised and is valued by the young people themselves. It is much harder to show if a 16-year-old is more inquisitive, resilient, imaginative, self-aware and motivated than they were, say, two years ago, than it is to show whether they achieve a certain percentage in a knowledge-based test but it is important that we try. Unless such performance measures are developed, GCSE and A Level results will continue to be the tail that wags the dog and IQ will continue to defeat EQ.

Our education system needs to be rebuilt - starting with great teachers changing how they teach - around the following core principle: that the purpose of education is to prepare young people for life after school, to help them develop the mental, emotional, social and cultural resources they need in their armoury in order to enjoy challenge and cope with uncertainty and pressures.

CHAPTER NINETEEN

The talent myth

In 2002, Malcolm Gladwell wrote an article for The New Yorker called 'The Talent Myth' which criticised America's largest and most prestigious management-consulting firm, McKinsey & Company, and their so-called 'War for Talent'. McKinsey & Company sent thousands of questionnaires to managers across the country before singling out eighteen companies at which the consultants would spend three days interviewing everyone from the CEO to human resources staff. As Gladwell explains, "McKinsey wanted to document how the top-performing companies in America differed from other firms in the way they handle matters like hiring and promotion".

The consultants were surprised by their findings. As they sifted through countless interview transcripts and questionnaires they grew convinced that the difference between winners and losers was more profound than they had realised:

"We looked at one another and suddenly the light bulb blinked on," the three consultants who headed the project—Ed Michaels, Helen Handfield-Jones, and Beth Axelrod—write in their book, 'The War for Talent'. The very best companies, they concluded, had leaders who were obsessed with the talent issue. They recruited ceaselessly, finding and hiring as many top performers as possible. They singled out and segregated their stars, rewarding them disproportionately, and pushing them into ever more senior positions. "Bet on the natural athletes, the ones with the strongest intrinsic skills," the authors quote one senior General Electric executive as saying. "Don't be afraid to promote stars without specifically relevant experience, seemingly over their heads." Success in the modern economy, according to Michaels, Handfield-Jones, and Axelrod, requires "the talent mind-set": the "deep-seated belief that having better talent at all levels is how you outperform your competitors."

-      Malcolm Gladwell, The Talent Myth, New Yorker, 2002

Gladwell disapprovingly concludes that "this 'talent mind-set' is the new orthodoxy of American management... it is the intellectual justification for why such a high premium is placed on degrees from first-tier business schools, and why the compensation packages for top executives have become so lavish".

One such company which prized the talent mind-set above all others was Enron. "Enron," Gladwell explains, "did exactly what the consultants at McKinsey said that companies ought to do in order to succeed in the modern economy: it hired and rewarded the very best and the very brightest - and it is now in bankruptcy. The reasons for its collapse are complex, needless to say. But what if Enron failed not in spite of its talent mind-set but because of it?" And this leads Gladwell to ask the central question: What if smart people are overrated?

Gladwell argues that hiring people simply because they have an MBA and are therefore 'smart' is not the secret of success; rewarding so-called 'talent' flies in the face of all we know about motivating people to get better and better at what they do and motivating them to such an extent that they want to keep on doing it.

The biggest problem with hiring and rewarding the smartest people is that the link between IQ and job performance is, as Gladwell says, "distinctly underwhelming": On a scale where 0.1 or below means virtually no correlation and 0.7 or above implies a strong correlation (your height, for example, has a 0.7 correlation with your parents' height), the correlation between IQ and occupational success is between 0.2 and 0.3.

"What IQ doesn't pick up is effectiveness at common-sense sorts of things, especially working with people," Richard Wagner, a psychologist at Florida State University, tells Gladwell. Wagner goes on to make an important point which has a bearing on what we've said about the need for schools to help students to develop their EQ: "In terms of how we evaluate schooling, everything is about working by yourself. If you work with someone else, it's called cheating. Once you get out in the real world, everything you do involves working with other people." So it is right that schools help students to improve their emotional intelligence (or what Wagner calls 'tacit knowledge') - after all, this includes team-working and empathy - because this helps them prepare for real life and, therefore, helps them achieve greater levels of success at work. And why is it important that young people leave our schools with team-working skills? Because, as Gladwell says, the best companies are those which promote team-working and cooperation:

"The broader failing of McKinsey and its acolytes at Enron is their assumption that an organisation's intelligence is simply a function of the intelligence of its employees. They believe in stars, because they don't believe in systems. In a way, that's understandable, because our lives are so obviously enriched by individual brilliance. Groups don't write great novels, and a committee didn't come up with the theory of relativity. But companies work by different rules. They don't just create; they execute and compete and coördinate the efforts of many different people, and the organisations that are most successful at that task are the ones where the system is the star."

Teachers need to help their students to develop emotional intelligence - skills such as team-working, empathy, motivation, self-awareness and social skills - because this will help them achieve greater levels of personal success and will help them prepare for working life. Moreover, to be emotionally intelligent is to have a growth mindset in which making mistakes is to be embraced as a sign of getting better, a sign of increasing one's intelligence.

What Enron did was judge: they used a 'rank and yank' system whereby everyone's performance was judged and scored - often based on spurious criteria and short-term goals. What Enron should have done was what the best teachers do: they should have created an environment in which its employees had intrinsic motivation, were skilled at what they did and were afforded the opportunity to learn and get better at it.

CHAPTER TWENTY

Conclusions

What have we learnt? We have learnt that teachers should teach not judge; they should provide their students with practice, training and method. In other words, they should create a safe and secure environment in which students view making mistakes not only as acceptable (rather than humiliating) but as evidence that they are making progress and becoming more intelligent. Teachers should have the highest expectations of their students, they should believe their students are capable of greatness and should instil this belief in each and every child in their care.

Teachers should praise students' effort but not their intellect or ability. Praising effort encourages greater effort and is a great leveller: everyone is capable of trying hard and can always try harder. Praising ability, however, leads to negative behaviours and often a decline in performance.

Learners should enjoy what they do and should complete tasks for the fun of it not for extrinsic rewards. Intrinsic motivation leads to continual improvements and long-term enjoyment; working for rewards leads to short-term improvements, a long-term decline in performance and a loss of interest in the task.

Everyone can get better at everything with enough practice. Practice should be purposeful: it should involve concentration, dedication and the right conditions. Purposeful practice involves thousands of hours but, with practice, anyone can achieve anything.

Emotional intelligence - which can be learned and developed over time - is a crucial means by which people can realise their full potential and achieve great success at school, at home and in the workplace. Learning transferrable skills such as team-work, independent study, motivation, self-awareness and empathy can significantly increase your chances of success. Schools must develop systems to help students become emotionally intelligent and the education system must discover ways of prizing students' EQs as much - if not more than - students' IQs.

We have learnt that 'talent' is a myth; that a high IQ does not mean someone will be more successful at work. Indeed, the correlation between IQ and occupational success is only between 0.2 and 0.3. Work is not about individual talent but about team-work and cooperation, about employees being emotionally intelligent. Schools need to catch up.

And we have learnt that geniuses are not born great. Some people may start life with different aptitudes but the only true 'gift' with which one is born is the gift of perseverance, hard work and resilience. It is a gift if one is able to learn how to fall and views each fall, not as a failure, but as a success because each fall is evidence that you are learning, it is evidence that you are getting better, it is evidence that you are growing your own intelligence. In other words, we have learnt that IQ is a myth.

End Matter

Bibliography

Binet, Alfred (translated by Suzanne Heisler). Modern Ideas About Children.

Bloom, Benjamin. Developing Talent in Young People. NY. Ballantine. 1985.

Deci, Edward L. Journal of Personality and Social Psychology 18. 1971

Dweck, Carol S. Mindset. London. Constable & Robinson. 2006. ISBN 9-1-78033-200-0

Ericsson, K Anders. et al. The Role of Deliberate Practice in the Acquisition of Expert Performance. Psychological Review ed.100. 1993.

Gladwell, Malcolm. The Talent Myth. New Yorker. 2002. and Outliers. NY. Little, Brown. 2008.

Goleman, Daniel. Emotional Intelligence. NY. Bantam. 1995.

Goleman, D., Boyatzis, R., & Rhee, K. Clustering competence in emotional intelligence: insights from the emotional competence inventory. (from R. Bar-On & J.D.A. Parker (eds.): Handbook of emotional intelligence.) San Francisco. Jossey-Bass. 2000.

Harlow, Harry F. Journal of Experimental Psychology ed 40. 1950

Harlow, Harry F. Current Theory and Research on Motivation. Lincoln US. University of Nebraska Press. 1953.

Hawkins, J. David et al. Communities That Care. San Francisco. Jossey-Bass. 1992.

Mayer, J.D., & Salovey, P. What is emotional intelligence? (from P. Salovey & D. Sluyter (Eds.), Emotional development and emotional intelligence: Implications for educators.) NY. Basic Books. 1997.

Petrides, K.V. & Furnham, A. On the dimensional structure of emotional intelligence. (from Personality and Individual Differences 29.) 2000.

Petrides, K.V., Pita, R., Kokkinaki, F. The location of trait emotional intelligence in personality factor space. (from British Journal of Psychology 98.) 2007.

Pink, Daniel H. Drive. London. Canongate. 2010. ISBN 978-1-84767-769-3

Stone Karen F. & Dillehunt, Harold Q. Self-Science: The Subject Is Me. Santa Monica. Goodyear Publishing. 1978.

Syed, Matthew. Bounce. London. HarperCollins. 2010. ISBN 978-0-00-735052-0

Free preview of
Teach: The Journey to Outstanding
and
Teach 2: Educated Risks

I'm often asked to send free copies of my books to charity auctions or to schools and colleges to act as prizes at staff training days.

When I ask colleagues which book they'd like me to send, they invariably reply: just send whichever is your favourite.

But choosing my favourite book is a bit like choosing my favourite child. Only harder.

When push comes to shove, though, I usually pop a copy of *Teach* in the post. *Teach*, and now its sequel *Teach 2*, are probably my favoured offspring because they say most of what I want to say about teaching and learning.

They were labours of love to write and, between them, the culmination of about three years' toil at the keyboard and many more at the whiteboard.

So if you've enjoyed this book and haven't yet experienced *Teach* or *Teach 2*, then I'd encourage you to do so and, by way of temptation, here's a little summary of what I cover in those two tomes...

TEACH

The Bayesian Method - we're better together

In *Teach* I began by recounting the story of the American submarine, the USS Scorpion, which was declared lost on 5 June 1968 and all its ninety-nine crewmen presumed dead. Although an immediate search was initiated, it was without success because, with a potential search area stretching out thousands of square miles, it was like finding a needle in a haystack. Accordingly, the USS Scorpion was struck from the Naval Vessel Register on 30 June.

Later that year, however, another search led by John Craven (no, not the one from *Newsround*; the Chief Scientist of the US Navy's Special Projects Division) employed rather different methods to try to find the vessel. Dr Craven polled a wide array of specialists in various fields for their thoughts of where the sub might be. Their guesses were then pooled into a single average guess. This method draws on the Bayesian theory that was first deployed during the search for a hydrogen bomb lost off the coast of Palomares, Spain, in January 1966. Not one of the experts' guesses was right but the average of all their guesses was surprisingly accurate and led the recovery team to within just 183 metres of the lost sub.

In *Teach* I said that I believed in the Bayesian method of improving teaching and learning...

In other words, I confessed that I did not possess a panacea, I did not have an elixir, a pill which once popped would proffer outstanding teaching and learning every time, and I didn't expect any of my readers to know the secret to outstanding teaching and learning either. However – like Craven's team of experts – together, I believed we would find all the answers. In short – and I

271

wanted this to be the motto of my book – I said that, as a teaching profession, we were better together.

The Pareto Principle - keeping the main thing, the main thing

The Nineteenth Century philosopher William James famously said that "the art of being wise is knowing what to overlook" and in *Teach* I advocated we should do just that. In other words, we should focus on the most important aspects of teaching and learning – the real drivers of change - and take small but sustainable steps forward. We should not adopt a different focus each week, whereby one initiative erases all memory of the last. Nor should we employ a 'one size fits all' approach that assumes that all aspects of our schools and colleges share the same strengths and weaknesses. Instead, we should ensure a personalised, common sense approach to improvement planning.

In *Teach* I also explained that economists have an 80/20 rule which they call "the law of the vital few" which is also known as the Pareto Principle – named after the Italian economist Vilfredo Pareto who observed in 1906 that 80% of the land in Italy was owned by 20% of the population. Joseph Juran developed the principle by observing that 20% of the pea-pods in his garden contained 80% of the peas. From this, we get the popular belief that 80% of the effects come from 20% of the causes. In business, for example, it is believed that 80% of sales come from 20% of customers.

It follows, therefore, that to achieve great teaching and learning in our schools and colleges we should focus on improving the 20% of things that create the most value. We'll get stronger results if we spend our time practising the most important things and even if we already do the most important things well, there is real value in practising them further because the value of practice increases once the thing being practised has been mastered. In *Practice Perfect* Doug Lemov et al say that to keep practising something once we've already mastered it is to develop automaticity, fluidity, and creativity.

There's another advantage to focusing on the main thing. As Ben Levin – the former Deputy Director of Education in Ontario – says, "One of the challenges in education is that the pizzazz is around having the seemingly new idea, whereas the real work is in making it happen... Having a great new idea is less important to success than getting ordinary things done correctly and efficiently".   The main thing has to be about what works in the classroom because, as Paul Black and Dylan Wiliam say in their book *Inside the Black Box*, "Standards are raised only by changes which are put into direct effect by teachers and students in classrooms".

The Big 3 - learning from the evidence

In deciding what the 'main thing' is, I believe in evidence-based practice. I believe we should use evidence gleaned from our own observations and from wide-ranging discussions with colleagues, as well as from quality external sources. In *Teach* I argued that there are three aspects of formative assessment in particular which I believe hold the key to unlocking the secret of great teaching. I called these three strategies the 'Big 3' and they were:

1. Pitch,
2. Questioning, and
3. Feedback.

These three strategies underpinned *Teach* because I was certain - and still am for that matter - that they are in the 20% of drivers, they are 'the main things' that if improved will lead to great teaching and learning.

The best of the rest - but no spoilers

In *Teach* I explored at length what the 'Big 3' - pitch, questioning and feedback - meant in practice. I also examined what 'outstanding' teaching and learning really looked and felt like. It's impossible to do justice to a 60,000-word book in this short introduction - and nor would I want to for the sake of my royalties! - but here is my best attempt at summarising the general tone and content of that book to aid your enjoyment and understanding of the text you now hold in your hands...

What is outstanding teaching and learning?

There is no silver bullet, no secret formula for teaching outstanding lessons – what works is what's best. The best thing to do, therefore, is to get to know your students by regularly assessing them and then to plan for progress by providing opportunities for all your students to fill gaps in their knowledge.

Learning is invisible and cannot be observed in a single lesson. A lesson does not exist in isolation; it is all about context, so it is better to think of a lesson as one learning episode in a long series. It does not necessarily need a neat beginning and end or to be in four parts and it does not need to prescribe to a particular style of teaching. For example, every lesson does not need to include opportunities for group work or independent study. A lesson can be meaningfully spent with students reading or writing in silence so long as, in the wider context of the series, there is a variety of learning activities.

The best teachers are sensitive to the needs of their students and adjust their lessons to the 'here and now'. Students work best for the teachers who respect them, know their subjects, and are approachable and enthusiastic. The most effective teachers are relentless in their pursuit of excellence and are able to explain complex concepts in a way which makes sense.

Outstanding teaching takes place when all students make progress over time. Students make progress over time when they are challenged and engaged. That is why the *Big 3* - the strategies I recommend you focus on in order to improve the quality of teaching - are: pitch (providing challenge); questioning (encouraging engagement); and feedback (leading to progress).

Learning takes place when certain cognitive principles are observed, including: factual knowledge must precede skill; memory is the residue of thought; we understand new concepts in the context of things we already know; it is impossible to be good at something without deliberate practice; and intelligence can be changed through hard work.

The 1st strategy in the Big 3: Pitch

Students are more likely to get better at something if they believe intelligence can be changed through hard work. The word 'yet' can be a powerful tool in the teacher's toolbox: "I can't do this... *yet*."

The best classrooms are those in which students feel welcomed, valued, enthusiastic, engaged, eager to experiment and rewarded for hard work. The way to achieve this is to prize effort over attainment and focus on progress (learning) not outcomes.

If the work is too easy, students will switch off; if the work is too hard, students will switch off. Work must be pitched in the 'zone of proximal development' – hard but achievable with support. If something's too easy, we rely on our memory instead of thinking (e.g. $1 + 1 =$); if it's too hard, we run out of processing power (e.g. $46 \times 237 =$) and stop thinking; if it's challenging but achievable and we are successful, our brains reward us with a dose of dopamine which is pleasurable and binds neurones together creating memories. This is learning.

Desirable difficulties make information harder to encode (learn initially) but easier to retrieve later. This leads to deeper learning. We achieve desirable difficulties by:

spacing learning apart with increasingly long gaps; interleaving topics rather than finishing one topic then moving onto another; testing frequently – using low stakes quizzes at the start of topics/lessons to identify prior learning as well as knowledge gaps, and to interrupt forgetting; and making learning materials less clearly organised so that students have to think hard about the materials (e.g. using a difficult-to-read font).

At its simplest, learning is concerned with the interaction between our environment, our working memory and our long-term memory. Our working memory is about awareness and thinking; our long-term memory is about factual knowledge and procedural knowledge. We can improve the speed and ease with which we retrieve information from our long-term memory and transfer it into our working memory (where we can use it) by making connections between new and existing information – applying prior knowledge to new knowledge.

Prior knowledge helps us to 'chunk' information together, saving precious space in our limited working memory, allowing us to process more information. For example, the acronym 'BBC' takes one space in our working memory whereas, without the prior knowledge that the BBC is a TV company, the letters B, B and C would take three spaces. Prior knowledge is domain-specific. We know BBC whereas people in Japan would know WMBC. They'd take one space to remember WMBC whereas we would take four spaces to remember W, M, B and C.

When planning lessons, we should focus on what students will be made to think about rather than on what they will do. We might, for example, organise a lesson around a big question.

We need to repeat learning several times – at least three times, in fact – if it is to penetrate students' long-term memories.

Tests interrupt forgetting and reveal what has actually been learnt as well as what gaps exist. Accordingly, we should run pre-tests at the start of every unit – perhaps as a multiple choice quiz – which will provide cues and improve subsequent learning. Retrieval activities like this also help students prepare for exams.

Information 'sticks', so to speak, when each lesson clearly articulates and is built around a simple idea – i.e. when the teacher is clear about the key take-away message from each lesson, which could be a question or hypothesis.

Information also sticks when we use metaphor to relate new ideas to prior knowledge and to create images in students' minds.

Information sticks when we pique students' curiosity before we fill gaps in students' knowledge (thus convincing students they need the information). This can be done by asking students to make predictions or by setting a hypothesis to be proven or disproven.

Information sticks when we make abstract ideas concrete by grounding them in sensory reality (i.e. you make students feel something). The richer – sensorily and emotionally – new information is, the more strongly it is encoded in memory.

Information sticks when ideas are made credible by showing rather than telling students something (e.g. experiments, field studies, etc. beat textbooks for 'stickability').

The 2nd strategy in the Big 3: Questioning

Classroom discussion – best achieved through artful questioning – makes students smarter because it makes students think. Questions should only be used if they cause thinking and/or provide information for the teacher about what to do next (in other words, we should avoid the 'guess what's in my head' charade). The most common model of teacher talk is IRE: initiation, response, evaluation. But it doesn't work very well. A better model is ABC: agree/disagree with, build upon, and challenge whereby students pass questions around the classroom. The Japanese call this *neriage* which means 'to polish' – students polish each other's answers, refining them, challenging each other's thinking.

Increasing wait time – the amount of time the teacher waits for an answer to their question before either answering it themselves or asking someone else – makes students' answers longer, more confident, and increases students' ability to respond.

Good questions are an expressive demonstration of genuine curiosity, have an inner logic, are ordered so that thinking is clarified and are a part of an ongoing dialogue. In open questions, the rubric defines the rigour. In multiple-choice questions – which, as above, are effective ways of interrupting forgetting – the options define the rigour. Effective assessment combines open and multiple-choice questions.

The 3rd strategy in the Big 3: Feedback

Feedback is information given to students about their performance relative to their targets. Feedback should redirect the student's and the teacher's actions to help the student achieve their target. Effective feedback: addresses faulty interpretations; comments on rather than grades work; provides cues or prompts for further work; is timely, specific and clear; and focused on task and process rather than on praising.

Feedback works best when it is explicit about the marking criteria, offers suggestions for improvement, and is focused on how students can close the gap between their current and their desired performance; it does not focus on presentation or quantity of work.

Feedback can backfire – it needs to cause a cognitive rather than emotional reaction – i.e. it should cause thinking.

Feedback can promote the growth mindset if it: is as specific as possible; focuses on factors within students' control; focuses on factors which are dependent on effort not ability; and motivates rather than frustrates students.

Self- and peer-assessment can be effective strategies because they: give students greater responsibility for their learning; allow students to help and be helped by each other; encourage collaboration and reflection (useful skills for life); enable students to see their progress; and help students to see for themselves how to improve.

Improving student' ability to self- and peer-assess can help raise their levels of achievement but self- and peer-assessment needs to be used wisely. Students need to be helped to develop the necessary skills and knowledge because research suggests that 80% of the feedback students give is wrong.

The only useful feedback is that which is acted upon – it is crucial that the teacher knows the student and knows when and what kind of feedback to give, then plans time for students to act on feedback (e.g. DIRT - directed improvement and reflection time).

And that, in a nutshell, was what I said in *Teach*. So good they made a sequel.

TEACH 2

Teach 2 is a sequel of sorts but it's not essential you've read the first book because you won't find any exciting cliffhangers being resolved in the pages of that book, or unravel any twisted plot-lines within the well-worn folds of its dust-jacket.

Instead, *Teach 2* says some of the things I forgot to say in *Teach* as well as some of the things I've learnt since writing the first book.

And one of the things I've learnt since writing the first book is that motivation requires: A destination to aim for – knowing what the outcome looks like and not giving up until you reach it; a model to follow – an exemplar on which to base your technique; a coach – someone who is regarded as an expert and who sets high expectations; regular checkpoints to show what progress has been made and what's still to do; regular celebrations of ongoing achievements; messages about upcoming milestones – being encouraged to "up your game" when achievements are within your grasp; and a degree of personalisation – the ability to make choices about how to carry out tasks in order to increase enjoyment and engagement.

What makes a great teacher?

Like master coaches, the best teachers teach in chunks: they show students the end result then break it up into its constituent parts. They don't expect their students to make vast progress overnight, they look for gradual improvements and suggest minor tweaks, they encourage their students to take one day at a time, to draft and re-draft, to slowly and incrementally get better. Great teachers understand the importance of repetition, of doing something – practising a skill, drilling for knowledge – over and over again until it becomes automatic.

Great teachers possess a vast grid of task-specific knowledge that allows them to creatively and effectively respond to a student's efforts. They want to know about each student so they can customise their communications to fit the larger patterns in a student's life. They are able to deliver information to students in a series of short, vivid, highly focused bursts. They don't necessarily speak in a dictatorial tone but they do deliver their instructions in a way that sounds urgent and clinical. They have a moral honesty and use their character and personality to great effect.

Expert teachers have high levels of knowledge and an understanding of the subjects they teach. They combine the introduction of new subject knowledge with students' prior knowledge; they can relate current lesson content to other subjects in the curriculum; and they make lessons uniquely their own by changing, combining and adding to the lessons according to their students' needs and their own teaching goal. They are therefore able to predict and determine the types of errors that students might make, and this means that they can be much more responsive to students.

Great teachers are relentless in their pursuit of excellence and their language with students is infused with this sense of urgency and drive. They need not argue about expected standards of behaviour. They achieve this in different ways – sometimes through the gravitas of maturity and experience, sometimes through warm, interpersonal interactions with every student. They have the ability to explain complex concepts in ways that make sense, they ask good questions and give really good feedback – however it is done, students feel that they are learning, they know where they stand and feel confident about the process.

The best teachers aren't great just because they deliver information, they're great because they create lasting connections. They're not about the words they say, they're about the way they make students feel. In short, great teachers know and care about their students. In short, great teachers make personal connections with their students. Although pedagogical and content knowledge is important, great teachers know that what matters most is how they apply that knowledge.

We refer to it as "teaching practice" for a reason – we are forever practising, forever striving towards excellence and expertise. And yet we will never master it. But great teachers never tire of trying new things, of taking risks. They experiment and evaluate; they try and reflect.

What is great teaching?

Aristotle once said that "excellence is not an act but a habit", and so it is with teaching: the foundations of a successful classroom are built of rules and routines, regularly repeated and reinforced. With this in mind, it is important that you firmly and frankly set out your rules on day one, immediately establishing who's boss – because if you don't articulate clear dos and don'ts before you start teaching then you will find it difficult to break the bad habits that inevitably fill the void. For example:

1. You should always have a seating plan for every class you teach, adapted for every classroom you teach in. A seating plan serves two purposes: first, it helps you to learn the names of your students because seating them where you want gives you a useful reference point; second, it helps establish your authority in the room by dictating who sits with whom, forbidding the formation of friendship groups – and in so doing, it makes clear that your lesson is a place for learning not for socialising.

2. You should learn your students' names as quickly as you can and use their names as often as you can. Ask students if they have a preferred name or (clean, sensible) nickname. You will be surprised how powerful this can be in making them feel valued.

3. You should try to strike a positive balance whereby you reward good behaviour or effort three times more often than you sanction unacceptable performance. Where possible, signpost the right actions as a means of highlighting and correcting the wrong ones. When you need to sanction a student, make sure you hold firm. Always follow the school's behaviour policy and do not allow students to negotiate with you or argue about the unfairness of life. You should also strive to be consistent and fair in what misdemeanours you sanction students for.

4. You should establish clear routines for the beginnings and ends of lessons - you can make or break a lesson in the first few minutes. You need to establish your authority and show them that your classroom is your domain. Make students line-up outside – at least for the first lesson – and only enter once they are silent, attentive, and have removed their coats.

5. You should plan lessons backwards - rather than looking at a blank sheet of paper and thinking up fun activities to fill it, you should start your lesson planning at the end – with the objective. By formulating your objective first, you are forced to ask yourself "What will students understand today?" (which is measurable) rather than "What will students do today?" (which is not). A lesson activity can only be successful if it enables students to achieve the lesson's objective in a way that can be assessed – whether or not an activity is fun is of secondary importance if not entirely irrelevant.

What do high expectations look like?

The higher the expectations you have of somebody, the better they perform. It follows, therefore, that having high expectations of students is not only a nice thing to do, it actually leads to improved performance. Having high expectations is simply about establishing a set of clear rules and routines. For example, teachers who have high expectations often operate a "no opt out" policy. In other words, a teaching sequence that begins with a student unable to answer a question ends with the same student answering the question as often as possible.

Teachers who have high expectations always insist that "right is right" - they set and defend a high standard of correctness in their classroom. For example, they use simple positive language to express their appreciation of what a student has done and to express their expectation that he or she will now complete the task. They also insist that students answer the question they have asked not a different question entirely. These teachers are clear that the right answer to any question other than the one they have asked is, by definition, wrong. As well as insisting on the right answer, teachers with high expectations insist that students answer the right question at the right time. They protect the integrity of their lesson by not jumping ahead to engage an exciting right answer at the wrong time. These teachers insist their students use precise, technical vocabulary.

As well as having high expectations of our students, we should insist that our students have high expectations of themselves because only by believing in yourself and in your own ability to get better will you actually do so. This means students should have a growth mindset and believe that they can get better at anything if they work hard. They need to accept that work has to be drafted and redrafted, following the maxim that if it isn't excellent, it isn't finished. Students should also seek out and welcome feedback. They should value other people's opinions and advice and use it to help them improve their work. Feedback should be given and received with kindness in a manner that is helpful and not unduly critical, and yet it should be constructive and specific about what needs to be improved.

What are the habits of academic success?

I don't believe in conspiracy theories. I do, however, believe in coincidence. So what's the difference? When you think about it, coincidences are perfectly rational because they express a simple, logical pattern of cause and effect. Take, for example, academic achievement. Several years ago while working as a deputy headteacher I interviewed fifty students in years 11 and 13 who had achieved high grades in their GCSE and A level exams. I found something spooky – an apparent conspiracy.

For example, all the students I interviewed had an attendance of more than 93 per cent; 90 per cent of them had a perfect attendance record. All the students I interviewed told me they used their planners regularly and considered themselves to be well-organised. As a result, all the students I interviewed completed their homework on time and without fail. All the students I interviewed told me they always asked for help from their teachers when they got stuck. Most of the students I interviewed were involved in clubs, sports, or hobbies at lunchtime, after school and/or at weekends.

All the students believed that doing well in school would increase their chances of getting higher paid and more interesting jobs later in life. Many of them had a clear idea about the kind of job they wanted to do and knew what was needed in order to get it. They had researched the entry requirements and had then mapped out the necessary school, college, and/or university paths. They had connected what they were doing in school with achieving their future ambitions.

Was it spooky that nearly all these high-achieving students had done the same things? Or was it a simple case of cause and effect: because these students shared these traits they went on to succeed? I believe it was the latter: it was because these students had attended school, were well-organised, completed work on time, and had an end goal in mind that they had achieved excellent grades in their final exams.

The cause was diligent study and determination; the effect was high achievement. As such, these young people can teach our students a valuable lesson - the recipe for success is to: Have good attendance and punctuality; be organised and complete all work on time; be willing to ask for help when you're stuck; have something to aim for and be ambitious; map out your career path and be determined to succeed.

One means of becoming better organised is to acquire effective study skills and the following study skills are proven to be particularly helpful to students: *Self-quizzing* is about retrieving knowledge and skills from memory and is far more effective than simply re-reading a text. When your students read a text or study notes, you should teach them to pause periodically to ask themselves questions – without looking in the text. Once they have self-quizzed, get your students to check their answers and make sure they have an accurate understanding of what they know and what they don't know. You should space out your students' retrieval practice. This means studying information more than once and leaving increasingly large gaps between practice sessions.

Elaboration is the process of finding additional layers of meaning in new material. It involves relating new material to what students already know, explaining it to somebody else, or explaining how it relates to the wider world.

Generation is when students attempt to answer a question or solve a problem before being shown the answer or the solution. The act of filling in a missing word (the cloze test) results in better learning and a stronger memory of the text than simply reading the text.

Reflection involves taking a moment to review what has been learned. Students ask questions such as: What went well? What could have gone better? What other knowledge or experience does it remind me of? What strategies could I use next time to get better results?

Calibration is achieved when students adjust their judgment to reflect reality – in other words, they become certain that their sense of what they know and can do is accurate. We need to teach our students to remove the illusion of knowing and actually answer all the questions even if they think they know the answer and that it is too easy.

How can we close the gender gap?

There are five key "gaps" in the educational outcomes of boys and girls – reading skills, reading for pleasure, maths performance, STEM uptake, and STEM careers. First, boys lag behind girls at the end of compulsory education in reading skills by the equivalent, on average, of a year's schooling. Second, boys are far less likely to spend time reading for pleasure. Third, and in contrast, boys perform better than girls in maths, although the gender gap is narrower than in reading. Fourth, there remain significant disparities in the subjects boys and girls choose to study, with girls less likely to choose scientific and technological fields of study than boys.

Finally, even when girls choose these subjects they are less likely to take up careers in related fields. This widens the gap later in life in the career and earning prospects of women. Furthermore, boys in OECD countries are eight percentage points more likely than girls to report that school is a waste of time. Meanwhile, in higher education and beyond, young women are under-represented in maths, science, and computing. In 2012, only 14 per cent of young women who entered university for the first time chose science-related fields of study, including engineering, manufacturing and construction. By contrast, 39 per cent of young men who entered university that year chose to pursue one of those fields of study.

Some people believe that the attainment gap between boys and girls is the result of biological differences. After all, there are more than a hundred genetic differences between the male and female brain. For example, according to Blum (1997), boys' brains generally have more cortical areas dedicated to spatial-mechanical functioning, whereas girls' brains generally have greater cortical emphasis on verbal-emotive processing. As a result, girls tend to use more words than boys and girls tend to think more verbally. On the other hand, some people believe that the gender gap can be explained by differences in attitude not biology; aptitude, they argue, knows no gender. According to many international reports on the gender gap in education – most notably perhaps a 2012 OECD report called *Closing the Gap: Act Now* – boys and girls, men and women, when given equal opportunities, have an equal chance of achieving at the highest levels.

In the final analysis, it doesn't matter whether we believe the gender gaps in education are the result of biology or attitude – or indeed, as seems most likely to me, a nuanced combination of the two. What matters most is that we teachers believe that the gaps can and should be closed so here are some possible strategies for closing the gaps in literacy and STEM:

Closing the gap in literacy

1. Schools should promote reading for enjoyment and involve parents (particularly fathers) in their reading strategies. Schools should provide students with opportunities to read around their own interests, and enjoy reading. Schools should have a reading strategy and should focus on the needs of groups of students who are more likely to fall behind – including boys – as well as the effectiveness of the school library in supporting these strategies.

2. Every teacher should have an up-to-date knowledge of reading materials that will appeal to disengaged boys.

Schools should have a library at their heart and the school librarian should play an important role in enthusing teachers with the knowledge of reading materials. Schools should be encouraged to invest in their library provision.

3. School libraries should target students (particularly boys) who are least likely to be supported in their reading at home, perhaps by working in partnership with children's centres to target younger families who most need support. Libraries should also encourage students to take part in important initiatives, such as the annual Summer Reading Challenge initiative.

4. Every boy should have weekly support from a male reading role-model. One boy in five thinks reading is more for girls than boys. This reflects the fact that mothers are more likely than fathers to support their children's reading, that mothers are more likely to read in front of their children, and that the teacher who teaches a student to read is more likely to be a woman. Many boys will be supported in their reading by males within the home, but for those who aren't, the recruitment of male reading volunteers is a helpful strategy for schools to employ. Schools could make use of volunteering initiatives to engage young men in the support of boys' reading.

Closing the gap in STEM

1. Ensure students have a solid foundation in mathematics because evidence shows that studying maths for longer increases the average grade in biology and chemistry more than studying biology and chemistry.

2. Help students to develop their spatial skills because, although it is stereotypical to say that women have poor spatial awareness and a claim without scientific evidence of genetic or hormonal differences between the genders, spatial skills are malleable through practice and

improving spatial skills has proven, in the US, to improve the retention of engineering students.

3. Emphasise the importance of communication skills in the practice of science and engineering, thereby changing the perception that individuals cannot be gifted or skilled in both maths and languages. The vast majority of STEM jobs involve team-work, which necessitates communication. Despite the importance of communication to engineering, interpersonal communication and collaboration skills are generally portrayed as the opposite of maths and science skills, implying that people are almost always more skilled in one than the other. However, research provides compelling evidence that communication skills are essential in engineering, and suggests that integrating maths and communication skills in engineering would be of particular benefit to female students.

4. Help students develop resilience because female students may feel apprehensive about performing on a spatial skills task because they fear that performing poorly will confirm the existing negative stereotype. This so-called "stereotype threat" may actually cause girls to perform worse than they would otherwise do and therefore the danger lies in the self-fulfilling prophecy. However, a mindset shift – whereby girls are presented with experiential accounts of the origins of stereotypes – can have measurable positive consequences to combat this downward spiral. Several popular studies by Professor Carol Dweck have found that focusing on the power of practice rather than innate talent can be a key motivator for students and teaching the power of a growth mindset allows girls to perform better, even when they understand the stereotypes against them.

5. Give female students an active expert role whereby they answer questions, make comments, teach others and express their own voice through presentation because it will make them feel like they belong to the expert group. Since this feeling of belonging is what girls

often lack in STEM fields, active expert roles can help girls in particular to enhance their sense of belonging to their classmates and to the learning material.

6. Have a clear marking policy that ensures constructive feedback is given to help girls to properly gauge their success since a study by sociologist Shelley Correll found that girls need a better picture of where they stand in maths and science classes than do boys because otherwise they will use their biased self-assessment. The implications of these studies are that marks and test scores in maths and science must be better explained to students and feedback must be clearer and more constructive.

7. Re-evaluate the use of group work because, while group work has often been encouraged as an exercise to build team-work and communication skills, a study on interpersonal communication which focused on gender and engineers versus non-engineers found that "engineering males were more likely than other groups to draw negative conclusions about speakers who engaged in self-belittlement by admitting to difficulties or mistakes – particularly with technological issues". Also, Debbie Chachra, in an editorial entitled *The Perils of Teamwork*, argues that asking students in STEM classes to work in teams does not have the desired supportive effect. Since school students have various levels of experience, they tend to divide based on skill-sets and self-efficacy. As such, girls are often given less technical and more managerial tasks. This can perpetuate a vicious cycle, says Chachra, to make girls feel that they do not belong in the maths and science fields.

How do students learn?

Students come to the classroom with preconceptions about how the world works. If their initial understanding is not engaged, they may fail to grasp any new concepts or information that is taught, or they may remember them for the purposes of a test but then revert to their preconceptions when outside the classroom. In order to develop competence in an area of inquiry, students must have a deep foundation of factual knowledge, understand facts and ideas in the context of a conceptual framework, and organise knowledge in ways that facilitate retrieval and application. A meta-cognitive approach to instruction can help students learn to take greater control of their own learning by defining learning goals and monitoring their progress in achieving them.

In order to help students become experts, we need to draw out and work with the pre-existing understanding they bring with them. This means actively inquiring into students' thinking, and creating classroom tasks and conditions under which student thinking can be revealed. We also need to teach less subject matter but cover the content we do teach in greater depth, providing many examples in which the same concept is at work and by so doing proffer a firm foundation of factual knowledge. And we need to teach meta-cognitive skills in order to enhance student achievement and develop students' ability to learn independently.

One practical means of doing this is to use constructive alignment, a concept that derives from cognitive psychology and constructivist theory and recognises the importance of linking new material to experiences in the learner's memory, as well as extrapolating that material to possible future contexts – connecting the learning, showing the bigger picture. The teacher makes a deliberate alignment between the planned learning activities and the learning outcomes. This is a conscious effort to provide the learner with a clearly defined goal, a well-designed learning activity that is appropriate for the task, and well-designed assessment criteria for giving feedback to the learner once they've completed that task. In constructive alignment you start with the outcomes you want students to learn, and then align teaching and assessment to those outcomes.

Constructive alignment marries well with the SOLO taxonomy which stands for "structure of observed learning outcomes" and helps to map levels of understanding that can be built into intended learning outcomes and create assessment criteria or rubrics. It consists of five levels of understanding: 1. Pre-structural: a student hasn't understood the point and offers a simple – incorrect – response; 2. Uni-structural: a student's response only focuses on one relevant aspect; 3. Multi-structural: here, a student's response focuses on several relevant aspects but these are treated independently of each other; 4. Relational: here, the different aspects seen at the multi-structural level have become integrated to form a coherent whole; 5. Extended abstract: the integrated whole is now conceptualised at a higher level of abstraction. As students move up the five levels, their understanding grows from surface to deep to conceptual. The SOLO taxonomy also helps develop a growth mindset because students come to understand that declarative and functioning learning outcomes are the result of effort and the use of effective strategies rather than the result of innate ability.

How can we teach students to transfer their learning?

The ability to extend what has been learned in one context to new contexts is called 'transfer' and helping our students to develop this skill is vital if we want them to be able to transfer what we teach them in one lesson to another lesson on a similar topic but this ability to transfer is not necessarily automatic; rather, we need to teach it. Several critical features of learning can affect a student's ability to transfer what they have learned. To help students to develop 'transfer' we should: allow a sufficient amount of time for initial learning to take place; plan for distributed – or spaced – learning and engage in deliberate practice; make sure students are motivated to learn by planning work with sufficient challenge; teach information in multiple, contrasting contexts and/or in abstract form; teach metacognition so that students become expert at monitoring and regulating their learning.

Why do students crave variety?

Students are more likely to want to learn - and to *actually* learn - if their interest is piqued by newness, by the extraordinary, by the unfamiliar. Students crave variety; they need lessons to surprise them, to excite them, to ignite new sparks and pose new questions. They need lessons to unsettle them, too; to discomfort and challenge them, not bore them with a Groundhog Day feeling of de ja vu all over again. In short, we all grow tired of repetition, of the predictable and prosaic, of the monotonous and mundane, and we all need a frequent frisson of freshness in our lives. But surely not all lessons can provide novelty value? Well, no, but in order to make ideas 'stick' we need to make them tangible because students find it hard to care about or understand abstract concepts. If we ground an abstract concept in sensory reality and thus engage our students' emotions, our students are made to care about something, they are made to feel something and this is an important part of the learning process because when we are exposed to new information, we process it then attempt to connect it to existing information (in other words, we try to assimilate new knowledge with prior knowledge). The richer – sensorily and emotionally – the new information is, and the deeper the existing information is engrained, the stronger we will encode the new information in our long-term memories.

Ensuring our lessons provide variety and novelty, therefore, helps to appeal to students' senses *and* engage their emotions - if nothing else, simply by piquing their interest in something out of the ordinary, we're waking them up, shaking them up and making them think - and therefore the information we teach them is more likely to be retained over the long-term. So try something new. Bring learning to life with something exciting, something different, something surprising. Be assured, however, that providing variety and novelty in this way - that teaching lessons which students will never forget - doesn't mean your lessons can't follow a regular, familiar structure - my plea relates *only* to your teaching methods *not* your lesson structure. In other words, in order to engage students and make lessons memorable, I'm suggesting you aim to use varied and novel teaching approaches and strategies (activities or tasks, if you like) but that you continue to organise the learning in a logical - perhaps even predictable - way. So...

What's the secret of great lesson planning?

You can't prescribe the unpredictable; you can't dictate differentness but you can derive a set of fundamental rules or guidelines for what constitutes an effectively *planned* and organised lesson because even unique lessons which are full of surprise possess some common elements of design and obey a set of shared principles - what we might call our 'design for learning' or our 'five point plan':

Firstly, well-planned lessons **connect the learning** in three ways: 1. They articulate a clear learning goal that students understand - in other words, students are told where the lesson is headed. 2. They articulate a clear purpose for the learning - in other words, students are told why the learning goal is important and why they are learning what they're learning. 3. They ensure that students' starting points (what they already know as well as their misconceptions) are identified through pre-tests.

Secondly, well-planned lessons **personalise the learning**. They ensure that the learning is tailored to meet individual needs and to match individual skills, interests, and styles. They also ensure that this diagnostic data about students' starting points and misconceptions (both that gathered from pre-tests and that gleaned from ongoing assessments) is used to inform the lesson planning process.

Thirdly, well-planned lessons **grab students' attentions**. They ensure that the learning activities get and maintain students' attentions from the very beginning by using sensory 'hooks' and by ensuring that the learning is appropriately paced, and appropriately varied and challenging.

Fourthly, well-planned lessons **teach less and learn more**. They ensure that students acquire the necessary experiences, knowledge and skills to meet the learning goals but in so doing they remember that less is more: they cover a smaller amount of curriculum content so that they can explore it in greater depth and detail - and from a range of different perspectives - than they would be able to achieve if they attempted to 'get through' more content.

Finally, well-planned lessons **make time for students to reflect**. They provide students with regular opportunities to reflect on their progress, to revise their thinking and to re-draft their work, acting on the formative feedback they receive from teacher-, peer- and self-assessments.

What motivates students?

The first step towards encouraging students to produce high-quality work is to set assessment tasks which inspire and challenge them and which are predicated on the idea that every student will succeed, not just finish the task but produce work which represents personal excellence. The most effective assessment tasks offer students an opportunity to engage in genuine research not just research invented for the classroom. A student's finished product needs a real audience and the role of the teacher is to help students to get their work ready for the public eye. This means there is a genuine reason to do the work well, not just because the teacher wants it that way. Not every piece of work can be of genuine importance but every piece of work can be displayed, presented, appreciated, and judged.

Assessment tasks work best when they are structured in such a way as to make it difficult for students to fall too far behind or fail. Tasks also work best when they are broken into a set of clear components so that students have to progress through checkpoints to ensure they are keeping up. Good tasks have in-built flexibility to allow for a range of abilities. Assessment tasks work best when they have in-built rubrics which make clear what is expected of each student at each stage of development. In other words, the rubric spells out exactly what components are required in the assignment, what the timeline for completion is, and on what qualities and dimensions the work will be judged.

The best way of delivering all of the above is project-based learning which can also help students to become more creative, more positive and more independent. It helps if project-based learning forms part of the whole school culture, if it is common practice across all classes and year groups, and if it is the accepted mode of learning. There are three strands of project-based learning well worth remembering - indeed, in many ways, these three are the cornerstones of effective projects:

1. A genuine outcome - if students are to commit time and effort to their project, they need to know that there is a real audience and means of exhibition for their work. In other words, if students know their work is going to be put on public display, there to be critiqued by members of the public, including their family and friends and not just their teachers, they are more likely to work hard and produce their best quality work.

2. Multiple drafts - in real life, when the quality of work matters, we rarely submit our first attempt at something but in many schools students hand in their first attempt at something, have it marked and returned, then discard it before moving on to the next task. Project-based learning enables students to positively engage with the drafting and redrafting process, and encourages them to make time for and recognise the importance of polishing work until such a time as it represents their very best efforts. Producing multiple drafts is not only a great way of teaching students about the real life importance of redrafting, but it also provides great opportunities for personalised assessment.

3. *Ongoing assessment* - producing multiple drafts helps students to engage in formative assessment, learning from feedback and making gradual improvements. Re-drafting also enables students to learn from each other by critiquing each other's work. Regarded in this way, critique, - far from being a distraction or added burden - becomes integral to the learning process. Critique can become a lesson in its own right, providing opportunities for the teacher to give instruction, to introduce or refine concepts and skills. Such lessons can also bring students' misunderstandings to the fore, enabling the class to respond en masse.

Project-based learning also works best when students regard the project as personally meaningful and when it fulfils an educational purpose - in other words, when it is an integral part of the curriculum. A project can be made personally meaningful if teachers begin by triggering students' curiosity. In other words, at the start of the first lesson on the project, the teacher uses a 'hook' to engage students' interest and initiate questioning. A project can also be made personally meaningful to students if the teacher poses a big question which captures the heart of the project in clear, compelling language, and which gives students a sense of purpose and challenge. A project can be made personally meaningful to students if students are given some choice about how to conduct the project and present their findings. Indeed, the more choice, the better.

A project can fulfil an educational purpose if it provides opportunities to build metacognition and character skills such as collaboration, communication, and critical thinking, which will serve students well in the workplace as in life. A project can also fulfil an educational purpose if students conduct a real-life inquiry, rather than finding information in textbooks or on the Internet then making a poster. A project can also fulfil an educational purpose if it makes learning meaningful by emphasising the need to create high-quality products and performances through the formal use of feedback and drafting. A project can fulfil an educational purpose if it ends with a product being presented to a real audience. Work is more meaningful when it is produced not only for the teacher or the test but for a real public audience. This makes students care more about the quality of their work.

What is 'vision' and why does it matter?

A vision makes explicit what an organisation stands for and what its people want it to achieve; it binds people (staff, students, governors, the community, employers, and so on) together in the pursuit of a common goal and reminds them why they do what they do every day. A vision provides a focus for decision-making and conveys a picture of what the future will look like. An effective vision is desirable in that it appeals to long-term interests. It is feasible in that it comprises realistic, attainable goals and is focused in that it is clear enough to provide guidance in decision making. An effective vision is also flexible in that it is general enough to allow individual initiative and alternative responses in light of changing conditions. It is also communicable. In other words, it is easy to communicate and can be successfully explained within five minutes.

The vision needs to frame every conversation and speech, needs to focus every meeting, and inform every decision. It needs to be used like a mantra. It will remind people of their ultimate goal and refocus them on what's most important; it will convince them that they are playing a crucial role in helping to make the organisation's vision a reality and reassure them that they are helping to shape the future.

Is teaching a profession?

One such vision statement I worked with recently had at its heart the simple words "to ensure every student is challenged, engaged and making progress every day" because I wanted to strip away the sometimes distracting detail and focus on what fundamentally matters most in teaching - and if we cannot say that every student is challenged (i.e. doing something difficult), engaged (i.e. actively involved in the learning process and thinking for themselves), and making progress (i.e. learning something new each lesson and making progress over time) then we must surely have failed in our duty as educators.

For me, the most important words in that particular vision statement were 'all' and 'every day' because I firmly believed that it was not acceptable if some of our students were challenged but others were stuck or bored, it was not acceptable if some of our students were engaged but others were switched off or distracted, and it was not acceptable if some of our students were making progress but others were not learning anything at all. Equally, it was not acceptable if the lessons that were observed (be that formally or through learning walks, peer observations or coaching) were 'good' or 'outstanding' because they were an artificial showcase of what we could do when we tried really hard but what our students actually experienced on a normal day – and therefore what they experienced day in, day out, most of the time - was less than 'good'.

As such, that vision was really about achieving consistency and so at the beginning of that particular journey I had to wrestle with two apparently contradictory beliefs. On the one hand, I believed that teaching was a profession (as opposed to a job) and that teachers were professionals (as opposed to workers). It followed, therefore, that teachers should be afforded autonomy in the classroom rather than be dictated to by senior leaders. On the other hand, I believed that – in order to raise students' aspirations and improve outcomes – sometimes, senior leaders needed to balance their defence of teacher autonomy with their need to achieve school-wide consistency; sometimes, leaders needed to insist upon every teacher following a set of common working practices so that they could be sure that every student was in receipt of the same high standards of teaching because a child's birth should not be her destiny.

I ended my infernal internal debate by concluding that the level of autonomy afforded to teachers was dependent (to some extent, and notwithstanding their own professional experience and expertise) on where their school was along the path to excellence – schools needed to *tighten up* the constraints on autonomy in order to be 'good' but could *loosen* those constraints in order to become 'outstanding'. I also decided that we needed greater clarity around what, when schools did indeed loosen the constraints on autonomy, it really meant to be an autonomous teacher. Specifically, I decided we needed to stop thinking of autonomy in terms of individual, idiosyncratic habits of working alone and start thinking of autonomy in terms of collective autonomy, the kind of autonomy afforded to professionals in medicine and law and aviation.

Individual autonomy and professionalism were not, I decided, synonymous. Indeed, to be a professional was to work *as part of* a profession not to work idiosyncratically and in isolation. But perhaps collective autonomy and professionalism could become synonymous. Perhaps we could conflate the two terms and begin talking in terms of *professional autonomy* - and professional autonomy was about working with colleagues in a way that led to greater consistency and coherence, in a way that led to the same high standards of education being afforded to every student no matter their individual context. Professional autonomy was about supporting and challenging one another to ensure we all improved by reflecting on feedback, by analysing our impact, by engaging in deliberate practice and by learning from our mistakes just as we expected our students to do. And professional autonomy was also about working collectively to build the solid foundations of teaching, groundworks constructed of rules and routines regularly repeated and reinforced so that they come to be regarded as the 'standard operation' in every classroom in every corridor of the school.

Should teachers take risks?

Great teaching is about passing on established wisdom - to quote Matthew Arnold, "the best which has been thought and said". But it is about much more than this. It also establishes new meanings and forges new connections and understandings, it changes the self and the world around the self. Education is a social art - it is more than mere production or reproduction and if we view education in these terms then we must move beyond compliance and encourage greater risk-taking and greater experimentation in education. Education cannot conform, it cannot inflexibly follow a prescription if it is to focus on how we help our students to engage with, and thus come into, the world.

Teaching must have meaning beyond the facilitation of learning. In other words, teaching must have a meaning that comes from the outside and brings something radically new - it emancipates students. Students learn from the practices in which they take part, they learn by participating in a shared experience. It is only through the act of learning and engaging in classroom activity that they discover the meaning of the world; meaning cannot be derived without this interaction.

So if we are to regard education as a means of creating new knowledge and not just of 'passing on' existing knowledge then we must move beyond notions of compliance and conformity and encourage greater risk-taking and experimentation in the classroom. Teachers cannot inflexibly follow a lesson plan if they are to focus on helping students to engage with, and thus come into the world. And the purpose of education is, if nothing else, to help our students find their own way into the world and to create their own new beginnings, to forge their own futures.

It is, if you like, the ultimate pedagogical oxymoron: risk-taking within a set of rules and routines; freedom within a framework; autonomy within a profession. Or, to put it another way, it is an educated risk.

Is neuroscience the next cargo cult in education?

There's a now famous story about the residents of an island in the South Pacific who, during the Second World War, saw heavy activity by US planes bringing in goods and supplies for soldiers. For most islanders, this was the first time they'd seen this kind of technology. When the war ended, naturally so did the cargo shipments. Confused and keen to see the activity resume, some islanders built fake air-strips with wooden control towers, bamboo radio antennae, and fire torches instead of landing-lights. They believed this would attract more US planes carrying precious cargo. The physicist Richard Feynman used this event to coin the phrase "cargo-cult science". Just as the islanders' air-strips had the appearance of the real thing but were not functional, cargo-cult science refers to something that has the appearance of science but is actually missing vital elements of it. People involved in cargo-cult science use scientific terms and may even carry out research. But their thinking and – more crucially – their conclusions are scientifically flawed.

Neuroscience, it seems to me, is in danger of becoming the next cargo-cult. Although it sounds good, many references to the brain in educational books and articles are devoid of any real value and are what has come to be called "neurosophisms": the sophisticated but mistaken application of language associated with neuroscience. Neuroscience has certainly gained traction in recent years and people have become more interested in learning about how the brain works. This is, of course, a good thing and we should always encourage intellectual curiosity of this kind. It is partly what makes teaching a profession, after all.

The brain is fascinating and, although there remains much mystery about how it works, a lot more is now known that could influence the way we behave and, crucially, the way we teach and learn. However, if we insist on using neuroscience to explain common sense approaches to teaching, we are in danger of losing the debate by detracting from the real argument, by making the argument difficult to follow, or by making false connections between behavioural and physical phenomena.

Therefore, I would encourage you to question teaching advice that's presented as neuroscience and to be wary of salesmen who want your school to sign up to a programme backed by research from the field of cognitive neuroscience, especially if it comes adorned with pretty brain scans.

You can make a quick start simply by asking the following questions whenever you come across an article, book or marketing flyer that cites neuroscience: 1. Can I replace the word "brain" with the word "student" (or similar) without losing any of the meaning? 2. Is the advice being presented new or is it the product of common sense and experience and something I have been doing successfully in my classroom for years? 3. Is the research that is cited in support of the argument, psychological, educational or behavioural? If so, there is no need to defer to neuroscience.

About the author

M J Bromley is an experienced education leader, writer, consultant, speaker and trainer.

You can find out more about him and read his free blog at
www.bromleyeducation.co.uk

@mj_bromley

@mjbromley

/mjbromleytl

/mattbromleytl

Also by the author

Leadership for Learning
Ofsted Thriving Not Surviving
A Teacher's Guide to Outstanding Lessons
A Teacher's Guide to Assessment
A Teacher's Guide to Behaviour Management
The Art of Public Speaking
How to Become a School Leader
Teach
School of Thoughts
Teach 2: Educated Risks

As Editor
SPaG Book (by Matilda Rose)
Outstanding Literacy (by Matilda Rose)

EDUCATION

Supporting schools and colleges in the UK

Visit www.solutionsforschool.co.uk for more information

Follow Autus on Twitter.com/@AutusEd
Like Autus on Facebook.com/AutusEducation

AUTUS BOOKS
England, UK
www.booksforschool.eu
Twitter: @AutusBooks

Making KS3 Count First Published 2016
The IQ Myth First Published 2012

This Edition First Published 2016
Copyright © Bromley Education 2016

ISBN-13: **978-1535506564**
ISBN-10: **1535506563**

Printed in Great Britain
by Amazon